What

SEP 2 6 2006

TAROT

can do for you

About Barbara Moore

The tarot has been a part of Barbara Moore's personal and professional lives for over a decade. She is the tarot specialist for Llewellyn Publications. She is a Certified Tarot Reader through the American Tarot Association and has spoken at tarot conferences around the United States. Barbara's articles on the tarot have appeared in several tarot publications and in Llewellyn Publications' *New Worlds of Mind and Spirit* magazine. She has also sat on the *Tarot Journal* editorial board. Barbara's own education in the tarot has been—and continues to be—broad and enlightening. She has studied under renowned tarot scholars Mary K. Greer and Rachel Pollack, and she has taught the tarot to all manner of would-be tarot readers.

what
TAROT
can do for you

Your Future in the Cards

BARBARA MOORE

2004
Llewellyn Publications
St. Paul, Minnesota 55164-0383, U.S.A.

FIRST EDITION
First Printing, 2004

Book design and editing by Andrew Karre
Cover design by Kevin R. Brown

Cards from *The World Spirit Tarot* © 2001
by Lauren O'Leary
Cover photo © 2003 by Hannah Lynch
Illustrations from the *Universal Tarot* by De Angelis © 2000 reprinted
with permission of Lo Scarabeo.

Library of Congress Cataloging-in-Publication Data
Moore, Barbara, 1963-
    What tarot can do for you: your future in the cards/Barbara Moore.
        p. cm.
    ISBN 0-7387-0173-4
    1. Tarot. I. Title.
    BF1879.T2M653 2004
    133.3'2424—dc22   2003060623

Llewellyn Publications
A Division of Llewellyn Worldwide, Ltd.
P.O. Box 64383, Dept. 0-7387-0173-4
St. Paul, MN 55164-0383, U.S.A.
www.llewellyn.com

Printed in the United States of America on recycled paper.

To my sisters, Michelle and Joanne, who have traveled with me through the wondrous journey of life and shared my love of the tarot. Thank you for celebrating the magic with me.

Contents

Introduction

You sit across the table as a stranger flips over the cards, the images beckoning to you, drawing you in. And you wonder, "How does she know?" Or the pictures baffle you, and you think, "How does she weave a story from this jumble?" Whatever your reaction, you have come to the cards for a reason. You are at a crossroads; you are curious.

Many people ask, "Why does the tarot work?" Rachel Pollack, renowned tarot scholar, writer extraordinaire, and creator of the compelling *Shining Tribe Tarot*, addressed this question quite succinctly at a tarot conference in the summer of 2000. She answered, "I see you ask a two-part question. First: 'Why?' 'Why?' is a question that has plagued philosophers for centuries. It would be arrogant of me to attempt to answer that question here. The question's second part: 'Does the tarot work?' Yes." Ms. Pollack is right; the tarot does work. And you will learn how it can work for you.

The tarot, the "wicked pack of cards" as T. S. Eliot called it, is a wonderful divinatory tool—and much more. Just like the mysterious reader turning over the cards to reveal your life, as you turn these pages, you will be introduced to the rich and exciting world of tarot. You will learn many ways to use the tarot to enhance and enchant your life.

This is not a book of detailed card meanings nor will it provide instruction on how to make explicit, concrete interpretations. Rather, this book will teach you how to ask considered, probing questions of the tarot. It will also cover the archetypal, basic meanings of the cards and then show you how those meanings can be starting points for your own journey toward a fully formed understanding of the tarot. Finally, this book will cover a host of contemporary uses for the tarot.

Fortunetelling and divination are still the most popular uses of the tarot. In addition to discussing divination, we'll see how the tarot can help you create solutions to problems, add variety and depth to your meditation, and focus your spell working. Tarot is also an excellent tool for self-improvement and journaling. In this little book, you'll learn the benefits of each of these activities, see how to incorporate the tarot into them, and read an example of each process in practice. Because this book is a short introduction to all of these activities, a detailed recommended readings list is included to broaden your knowledge.

Perhaps most appealing about the tarot are the cards themselves. Selecting the right deck is an important and sometimes confusing venture. An entire chapter will be devoted to deck selection. If you already have a deck, though, you may want to take it out and refer to it as you read the next chapter.

The Tarot Deck

I f you have ever browsed catalogs or the shelves of stores that sell tarot decks, no doubt you've noticed other types of divination decks. Rune cards, medicine cards, angel cards, and others abound. While these divination decks are fine products and have their particular uses and appeals, keep in mind that this book refers to tarot decks. A tarot deck contains seventy-eight cards and has a very specific structure.

Seventy-eight cards may seem like a lot to take in. However, this complex deck conveniently breaks down into simple sections. The first main division is two parts: the Major Arcana (twenty-two cards) and the Minor Arcana (fifty-six cards). The word "arcana" comes from the Latin word *arcanus*, meaning secrets or mysterious knowledge.

The Minor Arcana

The Minor Arcana is usually very simple to understand because most people are familiar with the structure already.
Think of a pack of playing cards: four suits (Hearts, Diamonds, Clubs, and Spades) with each suit having ten cards
numbered Ace through Ten and three court cards (King,
Queen, Jack). The numbered cards in a playing deck are
called the "pip cards." Pips are dots or symbols that mark
numeric value; for example, the three of diamonds card has
three diamonds on it. In some tarot decks the numbered
cards have only pips on them, some have pictures showing
a scene that illustrates the meaning of the card, and some
have both. The Minor Arcana is structured just like a playing deck, with the addition of one court card for each suit.
The court cards of the tarot reflect their medieval roots:
King, Queen, Knight, and Page. The suits have different
names and symbols but still relate directly to the suits of
modern playing cards: Swords (Spades), Cups (Hearts),
Wands (Clubs), and Coins (Diamonds).

In addition to relating to playing card deck suits, the
tarot card suits represent different elements: Wands represent Fire or Air; Cups represent Water; Swords represent
Air or Fire; Coins represent Earth.

In the next chapter, we'll discuss more fully how these
elemental associations apply to the tarot. But you can
begin to get a sense of the card meanings already. If Coins
represent the element of Earth, then the cards in that suit
would represent "earthy" or tangible things. Water is often
connected with emotions, so the suit of Cups deals with

our emotional experiences. You will notice that Wands and Swords are connected with either Fire or Air. This relationship is dependent upon the creator of the deck.

The Minor Arcana translates as "the lesser secrets" and generally depicts events, situations, or people related to everyday life. An important characteristic of the Minor Arcana is personal control. That is, the Minor Arcana cards represent aspects of your life over which you have control.

The Major Arcana

The Major Arcana, then, refers to the "greater secrets" and deals with important life issues, milestones, or things of spiritual significance. These are aspects over which we have less control. The Major Arcana contains twenty-two cards, numbered zero through twenty-one. Just as the minor suits have elemental associations, so does the Major Arcana; it is connected with the element of Spirit. In addition to being numbered, the Majors are also named, generally, although not always, as follows:

0	The Fool	7	The Chariot
1	The Magician	8	Strength
2	The High Priestess	9	The Hermit
3	The Empress	10	Wheel of Fortune
4	The Emperor	11	Justice
5	The Hierophant	12	The Hanged Man
6	The Lovers	13	Death

14 Temperance   18 The Moon
15 The Devil   19 The Sun
16 The Tower   20 Judgement
17 The Star   21 The World

Variations from Deck to Deck

The description of the components of a tarot deck given above fits most decks. However, there can be differences from deck to deck. Some will have different names for the court cards, such King, Queen, Prince, Princess or Father, Mother, Son, Daughter. Some will denote the suits differently. Wands may be called Rods, Batons, or Staves; Coins may be Pentacles, Disks, or Stones. The Major Arcana cards are sometimes renamed with Death becoming Transition or The Hierophant becoming The Teacher or The High Priest. The numbering of the Majors is not always consistent—the most common change is switching the numbers of Justice and Strength. Some deck creators also add a card or two or three to their decks. This is uncommon, but not unheard of. If you've purchased such a deck, make sure you read the accompanying book to be aware of what cards are added and why.

Most decks do come with a book or at least a small booklet with key words for the meanings of the cards. Some you will find more useful than others. *This* book is not so much about specific, fixed meanings of cards as it is about providing guidelines to help you determine your own interpretations. In addition to guidelines, you will glean some ideas from the samples throughout and from the Card Meanings appendix. As recommended by the American Tarot Association, you are encouraged to develop your own meanings for the cards. Techniques for accomplishing this will be explored more later in the book, especially in the chapters on journaling and meditation.

Adopting and developing your own meanings may sound disconcerting—aren't there set meanings for the cards? Not necessarily. As a tool that works as a bridge between the conscious and subconscious, the tarot reflects the needs of the user. This idea as well as the few examples of variants amongst decks illustrate that the tarot is a fluid entity. While a bit bewildering, this is also part of the beauty of tarot. It is adaptable and can be personalized. You can make the cards and all the techniques described here your own; you can tailor them to meet your needs.

All this freedom can sound intimidating, but it is carefully contained by the structure of the deck. It is the structure that provides enough order to help navigate the chaos that is all too often our lives. A tarot deck's structure—the division of Major and Minor Arcana, of the pip and court cards, the numbering of the cards, the relationships between and among the cards—is central to how it works. But the deck itself has not always been used in the same way, rather its applications have evolved over the centuries. Where, you might be wondering, did the tarot come from and exactly how has it evolved?

History

Historical evidence exists placing the origins of tarot cards in the early fifteenth century in Italy. Although there are interesting theories and ideas about earlier, more mystical beginnings, historical data does not support these ideas. That is not to say they aren't true—just that we cannot prove them, or disprove them for that matter. Some of these theories maintain that the cards came from Egypt, India, China, or Jewish Kabbalists. There is particularly interesting theory connecting the ideas represented in the tarot with the philosophy of Pythagoras. It is also interesting to note that while the tarot has come down through the centuries virtually unchanged in terms of structure, these and other theories of the origins of the tarot have waxed and waned in popularity.

Here is what we do know. The earliest extant deck is the Visconti tarot, commissioned by the Duke of Milan in 1450. Decks and partial decks that exist from that time period are similar to the Visconti deck in that they are works of art commissioned by noble families. Sometimes family members were featured in the cards. These decks were used in a card game called *tarocchi* and the cards were called *cartes de trionfi* ("cards of the triumphs," or trumps). The game of tarocchi was popular for about one hundred years, before falling out of fashion.

The Visconti deck has the same structure as most decks do today, with the twenty-two Major Arcana and the fifty-six Minor Arcana. Modern printings of this deck, complete with gold foil accents, are available today. Most incorporate borders around the cards with the title of the card printed on it. However, when the cards were originally created, there were no borders or names on the cards. This was an incredibly iconographically literate age. The images on the cards would have been been instantly recognizable without textual cues.

Although there is some slight, suggestive evidence that tarot may have been used for divination during the sixteenth and seventeenth centuries, the use of tarot for divination became very popular in the late eighteenth and early nineteenth centuries. It was around 1781 that the French writer, scholar, and occultist Antoine Court de Gébelin "rediscovered" the tarot and recognized the archetypal images portrayed in the Major Arcana. After that, divination by tarot became very popular—a popularity it has enjoyed almost continually until the present time.

During the late eighteenth and early nineteeth centuries, tarot cards were mass produced and playing card games became more popular. Many of the cards were produced in the French town of Marseille. These decks had the same structure as the older decks, such as the Visconti Tarot. Like the Visconti deck, the numbered cards of the Minor Arcana of Marseille decks had pips on them rather than the full illustrations that became popular after publication of the Rider-Waite Tarot (see page 41).

The past twenty years have been something of a renaissance for the tarot. Not only are there many different decks to choose from, but also there are many wonderful scholars and teachers who have published wonderful books on interpretation and techniques. Tarot enthusiasts gather for regional, national, and international conferences. Classes are taught in various venues, from small New Age shops to adult continuing-education programs. Tarot techniques are being used in business settings and therapy sessions. All of this means there is more information readily available than ever before.

There are also more decks available than ever before. While a hundred years ago it would have been difficult to find many different tarot decks to choose from, today there are any number of decks in a great variety of art styles and themes. The number of decks to consider may seem overwhelming, but in chapter 8, we'll discuss different approaches to selecting your deck.

Not only are there many decks, there are many ways to incorporate tarot in your life. It is more than a game and it is more than divination. Divination, though, is one of the most popular and interesting uses, and it is divination that we will discuss next.

Divination

To know the future, to know which is the best path to take—divination has always fascinated humans and is the most common use for tarot cards. Many people think of consulting the cards as a form of fortunetelling, associating divination with the idea of predestination, the theory that the future is set and that humans are at the mercy of predetermined events. As the use of tarot has developed in conjunction with changing world views, though, these notions have lost their charm. The idea of foretelling a preset future is less appealing. Instead, more tarot readers are adopting the idea of personal responsibility and empowerment. The ways they read and use the cards reflect this change, allowing people to take a more proactive approach to their lives rather than a reactive, passive one.

This is not to say that we have total control over our lives. There are events, circumstances, and the actions of others that affect us. We can, however, choose how to respond to these things. We can gain as much knowledge as possible about situations and consider the consequences of the many different paths open to us. In that way, we can select, and thereby control to a greater extent, our own futures. As humans, with our myriad biases and baggage, we cannot always find on our own the knowledge we seek or understand the choices we face. So we turn to other resources. We talk to friends and family, to therapists, to spiritual advisors, and to our mentors. And sometimes we consult oracles, like the tarot.

Deciding to use the tarot as a tool is a powerful and important choice in and of itself, a choice you should understand clearly. Many people see tarot readings as comprising two elements. The first is fortunetelling or foretelling the future. Although the future is not set in stone, we can examine situations as they are and see the direction in which the future is tending. This is similar to fact gathering. The tarot can clearly illustrate a situation, including aspects of which we are unaware. The second element is divination. "Divination" comes from the word "divine." The divine, however you conceive it, usually includes the higher power that can guide you to your best possible life. The act of divination allows you to tap into that divine wisdom and love, to ask questions of it, and to incorporate it into your decision-making process. The combination of knowledge and wise counsel can make the act of creating your future much easier than it would have been otherwise.

Asking the Question

Searching for answers or information is not always easy. How many times have we ended frustrated Internet searches because we could not find the right keyword to bring up the desired site? How many times have people avoided relaying unpleasant information by saying, "Well, you never asked me"? The same can be true of consulting an oracle such as the tarot. Being able to ask the right questions is even more important than knowing exactly what each card means. Keep in mind, also, that there will be times when the tarot will not answer what we ask but will tell us what we need to know. We can make things easier for ourselves by realizing that getting the best, most useful answer depends largely on the question asked.

Since the future is not predestined, the phrasing of the question posed to the tarot becomes even more important than the desire to access information efficiently. The nature of the tarot's answer is influenced by the manner of your questioning. Easy questions no longer suffice when it comes to accessing personal power. Careful construction of the question is the first step in a useful tarot reading. In fact, sometimes the act of examining the phrasing will tell you as much about the situation and yourself as the oracle can. Imagine you are dating someone named Joe. The answers to the questions "Will I marry Joe?" or "Should I marry Joe?" really do not provide any insight. Instead, consider why you are asking these questions. Do you want to marry Joe? Why? If you are unsure, what are the issues that disturb you? Do you think that Joe doesn't want to marry you? Why? See how the nature of your questioning influences the answers?

You need to be very clear about what it is you want to know and why. Consider why you are even approaching the oracle about you relationship with Joe. What are your doubts and concerns? Do you have a clear sense of your goals in the relationship? If so, do you see roadblocks? Once you have reflected on the situation, you can construct a question to meet your needs. Returning to our example, let's say Joe is interested in marriage to you, but you are not certain you want to and are not sure why. There is a nagging doubt that you cannot identify. A possible question could be, "What is the root of my uncertainty about marriage to Joe?" The answer to that question could perhaps lead to another question. Once the issue is identified, you could explore possible solutions or actions in response to your newfound knowledge.

Let's change the scenario. In this one, you are certain that you want to marry Joe. Joe, however, has his doubts. He cannot or does not choose to discuss them. What can you do? Many tarot readers consider it unethical to read for or about other people directly without their consent. If Joe consents, then the two of you could form a question and consult the deck together. If not, then you must think more about what you want in the situation as it stands. If Joe is unwilling to commit, do you wish to stay in the relationship? If you are unsure, you could ask the cards, "What are the pros and cons of staying in this relationship?" Or you might ask what you can do to facilitate more open communication between the two of you.

Sometimes you won't have a specific question. Perhaps you feel a vague sense of disconnection, of imbalance. Everything may seem okay, but underneath the surface there is something missing or a bit off. Just as there are times when you may meditate or pray just to enjoy the sense of peace, to listen to the quiet voice that sometimes attends your spirit, there are times when the tarot has something to communicate. At these times, when analysis fails to provide a question and yet your intuition feels like it is hitting you over the head with a baseball bat, it is best simply to ask the cards, "What do I need to know right now?"

Once you have formed your question, you will need to organize the tarot in such a way that it can address your question. You will need to select a spread for your reading. While the question forms the foundation for the answer, the spread forms the framework or the shape for that answer. Understanding the spread's role in a reading and selecting the right spread are almost as important as understanding and phrasing your question.

The Tarot Spread

Most people are familiar with the scenario of shuffling the cards and laying them out in some sort of pattern (called a spread or a layout). This ordering of the cards provides a framework for the wisdom of the tarot and for the reader to form an answer. Each position represents a different aspect of the question; for instance, the card that comes up in one position may represent you, while the card that comes up in another position may indicate the possible outcome. Before you can deal the cards, you must decide whether to use a spread that is already created, such as the standard Celtic Cross (one of the most popular spreads), or design your own spread—or use a combination of the two.

Using a predesigned spread has advantages, especially for beginners who may feel they are learning too much at one time. If this is the case, by all means use a predesigned spread. There are books of spreads you can purchase and there are spreads available on the Internet, so there are many to choose from. You can browse through them and pick one that most closely matches the requirements of your question.

The Celtic Cross

Out of the many hundreds of spreads available to you, the one we will now discuss, the Celtic Cross, is the most often used. There are many variations on this spread, but the one on the facing page is very common.

Celtic Cross

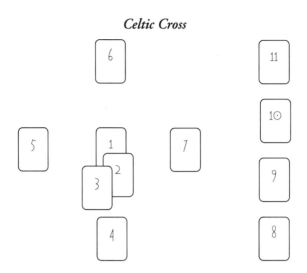

Briefly, here are the meanings of the positions:

1. **Significator (optional):** the significator is considered optional by many readers. The use of significators warrants its own section and will be discussed on page 32.

2. **You:** this card represents you in relation to the question.

3. **Crossing:** this card indicates the conflict.

4. **Foundation:** the card here will illustrate the basis of the problem or issue.

5. **Past:** here you will find significant influences from the past that shape the current problem.

6. **Present:** the present forces affecting the situation.

7. **Future:** the forces that will affect the outcome.

8. **Yourself:** this card is your self-image, which may be different from the "you" in card two. Self-image does not always reflect the inner you.

9. **Environment:** this is how other people see you in this situation.

10. **Hopes and fears:** this card illustrates either what you most hope for or most fear.

11. **The outcome:** this card indicates the probable outcome, if all things remain as they are at the moment of the reading.

It is easy to see why this spread is so popular: it can simply and clearly assess a problem, what caused that problem, and what the outcome may be. But, as with any pre-existing spread, it has limitations. The Celtic Cross is limiting in that it does not provide information on how to change the outcome. It presents a snapshot without giving tools for creation. It's all very well to have your fear identified, but how can you address it, change it, face it, etc.? The Celtic Cross spread can be a useful starting point. Once you've seen the snapshot of the situation, you can use the cards to gain more detail or insight.

First, if any card in the spread puzzles you, you can pull another card from the deck as a clarifier. Be clear about what you want clarified when you draw the card. Do you want to know more about the fear? Do you want to know how you can best overcome the fear? Remember, the question asked is important; if you are at all uncertain about what you are seeking, your reading might feel muddled or ambiguous. Another technique that can be helpful is to take the card in question and set it aside. Shuffle the rest of the deck and pull three cards, again being clear in your mind about what information you want from the tarot.

three-card spreads

If you find the Celtic Cross and the clarification techniques overwhelming or time consuming, another option is to use a generic three-card spread—simply laying out three cards in either a horizontal or vertical line or in a triangle, depending on how you label the positions. Some common variations are illustrated below.

Three-Card Spreads

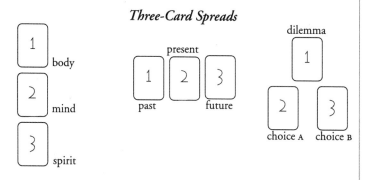

You can play with this variation, using any set of three that is appropriate to your question. The benefits of a three-card reading include being simple and quick to perform and interpret as well as providing clear answers to concise questions. Take Clara for example.

Clara

Clara, who works at home, is on her third day of a very intense project. The work, while within her realm of expertise, is somewhat new to her and she isn't making the progress she had anticipated. Part of her wants to stay at home and plow through the project. Part of her wants to set it aside and go out for the day. Going out would put her at least a day behind schedule. On the other hand, going out might help clear her head and renew her enthusiasm. She decides to do a quick three-card reading using her *World Spirit Tarot* deck.

1. **The dilemma:** The Fool
2. **Staying home and working:** Seer (Page) of Cups
3. **Going out:** Seeker (Knight) of Cups

Using the skills we've already discussed, we can see several things. A quick overview of the spread shows people, or aspects of Clara (the court cards and The Fool). There could be various aspects of Clara that are in conflict. Because Cups are prevalent, she knows that her emotions are very much involved. Now look at the individual cards. The Fool sums up the dilemma—Clara is at a crossroads. She knows she faces a decision, but because The Fool is a Major Arcana, it indicates that this seemingly simple decision will carry larger ramifications. On the side of staying home, the Seer of Cups shows a young woman sitting quietly and calmly while focusing on a simple chalice. The Seer is often someone in the early stages of learning a skill and is usually very dedicated and attentive to that process. On the side of going out, by contrast, is the Seeker of Cups, who is a romantic, someone who spends more time dreaming than doing.

This reading gives a clear, almost caricatured, illustration of the situation. At first glance, it may appear that this is all it offers. Is Clara any closer to a solution? Well, yes. She thought about the Seer and the Seeker and imagined herself taking on their behaviors. She did not admire the practices of Seeker—a person who spends more time in a fantasy world instead of channeling that creative energy into a useful plan. She could, though, admire the Seer with her sense of calm, attentive dedication. The Seer gives her a clue about how to make the best use of her time. Whereas

Clara was approaching her work in a frantic, oh-my-gosh-
I've-got-to-finish-it attitude, the Seer is calm and reflective.
Clara decides to adopt this attitude and give careful atten-
tion to what she has already accomplished.

creating your own spreads

Although many people use predesigned spreads, you may
find that, after carefully crafting your question, no existing
spread fully answers your question. The spreads that you
find may have too few cards or too many cards or just not
make sense to you. You are not going to use a predesigned
question, so why not design your own spread as carefully as
you crafted your question? By doing this, you can use the
number of cards you want and incorporate design elements
that are meaningful to you. This isn't as daunting as it may
sound, although it takes a bit of thought and analysis. A
well-formed question can make this process much easier.
Let's use an example from above: you want to marry Joe,
but Joe is unwilling to make a commitment. The question
is, "What are the pros and cons of staying in a relationship
with Joe, knowing that he doesn't want to marry at this
time?" An easy spread would be to lay one card to represent yourself (how you feel about this choice) in the center.
On either side lay out three cards to illustrate the pros and
cons. Or you can be more specific, as in the spread on the
facing page.

Nine-Card Spread

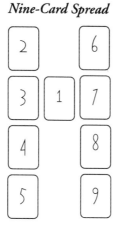

The cards each represent the following:

1. You

On one side lay cards to represent the following, if you stay in the relationship:

2. Your emotional needs

3. Your mental needs

4. Your physical needs

5. The possible outcome

Then on the other side lay cards (numbered six through nine on the diagram above) to represent the same, if you leave the relationship. This spread gives more specific information and indicates possible outcomes for each scenario. Note how Julie uses a similar spread to help make a decision.

Julie

Julie is a young college student. As with many students, finances are always an issue. As the beginning of the school year approaches, Julie finds herself faced with a dilemma. She has been offered a management position at the retail shop where she works. This would help with her financial problems. However, it would also mean that, in addition to a full class load, she would be working more than forty hours per week. She wants to know the pros and cons of both choices. Julie shuffles her *Nigel Jackson Tarot* deck and asks, "What is the largest aspect of the conflict in my mind and what are the pros and cons of each choice in terms of finances, achievement in course work, and extracurricular activities?" She lays out the following spread.

The conflict

1. Seven of Cups

Taking the job

2. **Finances:** Death

3. **Course work:** The Chariot

4. **Extra activities:** Queen of Swords

Not taking the job

5. **Finances:** Ace of Coins

6. **Course work:** Seven of Coins

7. **Extra activities:** Three of Coins

Julie's Seven Card Spread

Looking at the spread, Julie is surprised at all the Coins on the side of not taking the job—after all, aren't Coins all about money? Not really. They are about resources of all sorts, including time and energy.

Julie is not surprised to see the Seven of Cups illustrating the conflict, because she can relate to every element of the picture. The image on the card shows a figure staring at a night sky filled with chalices, stars, and strange firefly-like creatures. He holds his arms out and seems a bit awed by the sight of so many possibilities and perhaps even confused because the darkness and strange lights make it difficult to see clearly. This is exactly how Julie feels. She feels like she cannot see the choices clearly and objectively. Her emotions are engaged. On one

SEVEN OF CUPS

hand, she wants to prove that she can hold down a management job and succeed in her classes. On the other hand, she is eager to be involved in college life and all it has to

XIII Death

VII The Chariot

Queen of Swords

offer. On yet another hand, she dreads the thought of having no money to spend and incurring more debt.

Julie turns to the side representing taking the job. The Death card, representing the financial situation if she takes the job, disturbs Julie. It represents transformation and an ending—certainly a transformation of her current dismal financial state. But Julie is transfixed by the image of the skeleton on the card. All she sees are bare bones. She feels like she'd achieve a new financial situation, but at what cost?

The Chariot reflects the situation in terms of course work. The charioteer is definitely in control of the situation, but Julie knows that it is taking all his effort and a superb display of will to maintain control. Julie knows that achieving good grades does not come easily for her; she works hard to reach her academic goals. Taking the job would mean an even larger effort on her part. She is not sure she is up to it.

The Queen of Swords often represents a woman of sorrow, someone who has experienced great loss. Julie feels that giving up extra activities might make her resentful and regretful of her choices.

On the side of declining the job is the Ace of Coins, which is a new beginning. Julie isn't sure how not taking the job is a new beginning, as in her mind it is a continuation of her current situation. But when she thinks in terms of resources in general and not just money, she realizes that it can be a new set of priorities. If she makes her college experience her goal rather than money, then earning money is less of a driving force.

ACE OF COINS

The Seven of Coins shows a man relaxing while fishing. Unlike the charioteer, who is striving, this character is accomplishing his goal but is thoroughly enjoying himself while doing it. Julie thinks about the difference between plowing through her work just to keep up and leisurely enjoying what she is learning and doing.

SEVEN OF COINS

The final card, the Three of Coins, leads Julie to continue to consider the idea of rearranging her priorities. On this card, there is a man diligently working on a project. Julie's "project" at present is her education. The management position offers her management experience and would add to her résumé. However, it is not related to her long-term goals. Some of the

THREE OF COINS

extra activities she is interested in are directly related to her major and in the long run would help her achieve her career goals more than management experience.

In the end, Julie decides to not accept the position and to focus on her studies and long-range life goals. The decision isn't easy, as the idea of extra money and hence a more comfortable lifestyle beguiles her—just like the chalices and strange lights beguile the figure in the Seven of Cups. Death, The Chariot, and the Queen of Swords seems like a harsh lot and helps her focus on the realities of that path, allowing her to clear away the fantasies invoked by the promise of money. She starts appreciating the calmness and balance of the Seven of Coins and the Three of Coins. The vision of enjoying living and the unique opportunities of college life beckon. Julie jumps into her university experience without reservations.

One-Card Readings

If you are not up to a Celtic Cross or even a three-card spread, one-card readings are an easy way to practice. You still get to hone your question-asking skills and your knowledge of the cards without the added tasks of deciding on and interpreting a complex spread. For a one-card reading, you simply craft a succinct question that can be answered in one card, shuffle your deck, and draw a single card. If you are just learning the cards and don't have a question every day, you can simply ask, "What do I need to be aware of today?" Take John's case, for example.

John

John has a meeting at work this week about a possible project the company is considering. He feels very strongly about it and has what he thinks are compelling reasons for dropping the project. However, he is fairly new to the company and is still unsure of the dynamics of the committee. He wants to know what kind of attitude he should adopt for the meeting. Normally, being new to the company, he would be quieter, less assertive and vocal with his opinions so as not to make a blunder that may affect his future with the company. The expense and significance of the project, though, compel him to be more direct. From his *Universal Tarot* deck he draws the Queen of Swords. Because of his work with developing his own meanings for the cards, John knows that she is a person who has gained wisdom through direct experience. She is direct and truthful, sometimes sharp and blunt.

He decides to focus on his experience with similar projects for other companies, and, at the meeting, he will point out aspects that other committee members may not have considered. He will clearly describe various scenarios, how others tried to achieve success, and why those attempts failed. The Queen of Swords is also a very good organizer and problem-solver. John will therefore try to come up with variations on the project that may make it more successful. By embodying the characteristics of the Queen of Swords, John feels confident about his presentation and about benefiting the company with his experience. Like her, he has learned from experience and like her, he will be direct and truthful.

Significators

If you decide to study tarot further, you will read about significators, so we will discuss them here, briefly. In the Celtic Cross spread, as in many other spreads, there is a position for a significator card. This is simply a card that represents the querent (person asking the question). Traditionally, it is used as a focal point but is not usually incorporated into the reading or interpreted. Because of this, many readers no longer use a significator in this traditional manner. There are, however, two ways of using a significator can benefit a reading. We'll discuss them in detail on page 34.

A significator, traditionally, has been selected in one of four ways:

1. Use The Magician to represent a male querent or The High Priestess to represent a female querent.

2. Select a court card to represent the querent based on physical coloring and age, using the lists below.

3. Select a court card based on astrological sign and age, using the lists below.

4. Select a court card based on personality and age, using the categories and traits below.

AGE

Page: a child

Knight: a young man

Queen: a woman

King: a mature man

PHYSICAL APPEARANCE

Wands: fair skin with blond hair and blue eyes

Cups: light to medium skin with light brown hair and blue or hazel eyes

Swords: olive skin with dark hair and light eyes

Coins: dark skin with dark hair and dark eyes

ASTROLOGICAL SIGN

Wands (Fire signs): Aries, Leo, Sagittarius

Cups (Water signs): Cancer, Scorpio, Pisces

Swords (Air signs): Gemini, Libra, Aquarius

Coins (Earth signs): Taurus, Virgo, Capricorn

PERSONALITY

Wands: a fiery, passionate, energetic person

Cups: an emotional, creative person

Swords: an intellectual, logical person

Pentacles: a down-to-earth, practical person

Can you see the limitations in these methods? First and foremost, it takes a card out of the deck so that it cannot come up in the reading itself. This is particularly unfortunate in the case of using The Magician or High Priestess—two very important Major Arcana cards. Selecting a court card can also be problematic. In the cases of physical description and personality, not all possible combinations and subtleties are accounted for. The court cards usually represent one facet of a personality, so to pick one to represent a whole person is an oversimplification. However, you can try to select a card based on how the person feels in relation to the question.

Two other ways of selecting significators have gained in popularity and can actually be useful in terms of the reading itself. The first is to "let the deck" select the card. That is, shuffle the cards and use the top card as the significator. In this method, the significator can be read as another facet of the second card in the Celtic Cross, which also represents the querent. A second method works well with someone who is unfamiliar with the cards. Let the querent go through the whole deck and pick a card that represents him- or herself. This can provide interesting insight into how the person sees him or herself in the situation and can be read in conjunction with card eight in the Celtic Cross.

For example, let's say you are using a Celtic Cross spread and you let the deck pick the significator. The significator is The Empress and the second card, which represents the querent in this instance, is the Nine of Cups. You could say that in general the querent is a nurturing, creative person very much in tune with nature (a common interpretation for The Empress). The Nine of Cups often represents the attainment of desires or dreams. From the combination of these two cards, you could conclude that the querent is by nature a nurturing mother figure and that she is happy with this role.

Play with the various methods and see what works for you. You may wish to disregard significators altogether or you may even create your own method for selecting them.

Reversed Cards

Just as some readers use significators and some do not, some people choose to read reversed cards. Reversed cards are cards that show up in the spread upside down. Some people argue that the seventy-eight cards of the tarot already represent a full range of human experience and reversals just muddy the waters. New students of tarot often feel intimidated by learning yet another set of seventy-eight meanings. Others argue that using reversals adds depth and accuracy to a reading, that reversals are a way of fine-tuning your interpretations.

Again, this is a decision you must make for yourself. If you choose not to read reversals and cards appear upside down in your spread, simply turn them right side up. Many teachers (as well as the American Tarot Association) recommend that you first become comfortable with the cards upright before attempting reversed meanings. If you want to include reversed meanings in your readings, then you need to make another decision: how are you going to interpret reversals? Books that come with decks usually provide both upright and reversed meanings. Often there doesn't seem to be a coherent theory determining the reversed meanings; they may seem arbitrary. This method does indeed mean that you have to learn another set of seventy-eight interpretations. However, if you decide on a specific theory of reversals—one that simply and consistently modifies the upright meaning—your job is much easier.

Tarot experts offer many different practices for interpreting reversed cards. The most comprehensive work on this subject is Mary K. Greer's *The Complete Book of Tarot Reversals*. If you become at all interested in reversals, this book is highly recommended. For the moment, though, let's examine some simple possibilities to experiment with. The first and most obvious method is to say that the reversed card means the exact opposite of the upright meaning. Say the Two of Cups appears in your spread reversed. Your meaning for the card is union or partnership, often romantic. For the purposes of illustration, let's say this appears in a reading for Anna and Mike, keeping in mind that this example is oversimplified. The reversed meaning would then indicate dissolution of a union or partnership, so if Anna and Mike are dating, this could mean a breakup. If they are considering dating, it would mean that, although they may have a date, it will not become a union. Another technique is to say that a reversed card means that the energy represented by the upright card is blocked. Using the Two of Cups again as an example, you would say that the forming of a union or partnership is blocked and may be delayed in some way. Following our example, this could mean that Anna and Mike are trying to set a date, but cannot because circumstances won't allow it. However, in this method, we can assume that they will get together, just not necessarily in the immediate future. You can see how whichever method you choose for using reversals can drastically affect the interpretation of your readings. The best advice is to select your method very carefully and be consistent.

The Cards

This book is not about interpretation based on specific meanings. There are many excellent books available on that subject; possibly one came with your deck. There are also recommendations in the reading list. The guidelines and suggestions that follow will give you enough information to begin to understand what the cards mean. A discussion of basic meanings will give a framework. An exploration of more intuitive methods will help you expand and tailor the meanings for your own use. Finally, you will learn a technique for developing your own in-depth meanings.

basic meanings: the major arcana

In many ways the Major Arcana cards are both the easiest and the most complex cards in the deck. They are named as well as numbered, which gives you a clue right away regarding their meanings. They are also archetypes, images that are familiar to us in some way. Archetypes are patterns, experiences, or metaphors that recur in a culture, particularly through myths. We are most familiar with myths in terms of ancient or unfamiliar cultures. Myths in our own (American, twenty-first century) culture can be found in movies, literature, and popular culture. Just one example is the "wise old man" or The Hermit in the tarot. This figure, for instance, shows up in the *Star Wars* movies as Obi-Wan Kenobi and Yoda.

So, if The Fool turns up in your spread, without reading a single word about the card, you have an immediate idea of what it means by thinking about what you know about fools—the archetypal fool. A fool is someone who lacks knowledge or experience. Going a bit deeper, in medieval times, a fool was allowed to speak truths that no one else dared to utter. So you have a person who, while lacking knowledge or experience, is capable of keen insights, someone who is not afraid to say or do what he or she thinks, no matter how absurd or dangerous it may seem. The Devil card, as well, is not difficult to interpret. Most people think the devil represents evil and temptation. Strength, again, is fairly clear—a woman using gentleness and confidence to tame the wild beast. Keeping in mind that the Major Arcana are archetypes, we can see Strength as a metaphor for taming the beast within ourselves, for controlling animal urges that may not be in our best interest if acted upon.

Take a moment and pull all the Major Arcana cards from your deck. List them all and, based on the name alone (we'll get to the pictures later), jot down a few keywords that you would use in interpreting each card. Keep your notes from this and the following exercise. We'll be using them later.

basic meanings: the minor arcana

Although not always as obvious as the Major Arcana, the Minor Arcana are still fairly simple if you draw on the structure of the deck for guidance. Remember that each card belongs to a suit. Each suit has specific meanings and associations. Each card is also numbered; these numbers also shape the interpretation. By combining just this information alone, you can develop meanings for the cards. Here are few ideas commonly associated with the suits:

Wands: work or career, enterprises and projects, inspiration

Cups: emotions and creativity

Swords: challenges, intellect, rationality

Pentacles: the physical world, money, resources of all sorts, manifestation or completion of a project

The numbers, too, have a great many commonly associated meanings:

Aces: new beginnings

Twos: duality, balance, relationship

Threes: full expression of the suit

Fours: stability, structure

Fives: conflict or loss

Sixes: communication, problem solving

Sevens: reflection, assessment

Eights: movement, power

Nines: compromises, possibly stagnation

Tens: completion, ending of a cycle

Many people find the court cards challenging to interpret, and experts offer a variety of ways of interpreting them. One common method is to say that they represent either facets of the querent or other people in the querent's life. Each court card also belongs to a suit, so each presents a various aspect of its suit.

Pages: novices, a childlike expression of the suit—eager and enthusiastic but sometimes shallow

Knights: an adolescent expression of the suit—very often extreme and unbalanced

Queens: a mature embodiment of the suit or one who nurtures those qualities in others

Kings: a mature external expression of the suit

a history of meanings

All tarot decks are different, which is one reason it is difficult to write a book that provides meanings that apply to every deck. It is possible that the framework given above does not seem to work with your deck. If that is the case, you will rely more heavily on the intuitive approach described below and on the text that accompanies your deck.

The meanings above are based on what are often called "traditional" tarot decks. This is a misnomer, as the earliest (and arguably the most "traditional") decks were very different from what we are referring to here as traditional. Probably the most commonly known modern deck is the Rider-Waite deck, published in the early twentieth century. Rider is for William Rider, the name of the original publisher; Waite is for Arthur E. Waite, the man who designed the deck. The images were painted by a woman named Pamela ("Pixie") Colman Smith, so some people call this deck the Rider-Waite-Smith deck or RWS. Since the publication of the Rider-Waite, many decks have used the same basic meanings for the cards. Decks that do this are sometimes called "RWS clones." All the decks used as illustration in this book are Rider-Waite variations. Even if you are familiar with the Rider-Waite meanings, you will want to examine all the images in your deck.

An Intuitive Approach

By examining the structure and basic framework of meanings for the cards, you now have a foundation. You can add depth and accuracy by incorporating your intuitive and creative abilities by focusing on the images on the cards themselves. Let's face it; one of the most intriguing aspect of a physical tarot deck is the art. The images speak to us far more powerfully than names or intellectual associations. Much of life is about balance, so by incorporating both aspects of interpretation, you will get the most out of your tarot work. In this section, we will consider images and learn how to combine them with the meanings given above.

The intuitive approach is incredibly easy, though, ironically, it can seem incredibly difficult for some people. Pull a card at random from your deck and look at the picture. What do you see? What do you think it means? Sounds simple, right? Sometimes people get unsure about saying what they think a picture means. Perhaps they are worried about getting it "wrong" and their intuitions get blocked. If the first card you draw baffles you, continue drawing until you find one that resonates easily with you.

Let's try a Major Arcana example. You've pulled The Emperor from the *World Spirit Tarot* deck. You see an older man with an air of authority on a balcony of a tall building overlooking a pleasant town. He is holding a scepter in one hand; the other hand is held out in a sort of blessing over the town. Engraved on his balcony are symbols for the four suits of the tarot: a sword, a wand, a cup, and a pentacle. Just by the image, this card is about someone who has authority over a great many things. It appears that, under his leadership, the town has grown and is well organized and prosperous. The images of the sword, wand, cup, and pentacle indicate that he has used all resources at his disposal to create this situation. In short, this card speaks of leadership, ability, and stability. The Emperor card is usually numbered four. From our consideration of numbers above, you'll remember that the number four represents stability and structure.

For our Minor Arcana example, let's look at the Four of Wands, also from the *World Spirit Tarot* deck. This image shows a celebration, with a beribboned bower welcoming guests and many people dancing around a Maypole. The people in the card are celebrating

something as a community or group, such as the completion of a project or a holiday. If we combine this with the meaning of the suit and the number association, we can clarify a bit more. Wands are about careers or projects. Fours are about stability and structure. This card, then, is a celebration in honor of the successful completion of a project. See how easy this can be?

At this point, you may want to go through your deck, dividing the cards into piles, separating them by suit and putting them in numerical order. Go through the cards fairly quickly, looking at the picture and combining it with the associations from its suit and number and writing down your first impressions of the meaning. After doing this, you might want to try a simple three-card spread. If you are unsure what to ask or which spread to use, try doing the body-mind-spirit three-card spread (page 21, illustration), simply asking the cards to give you a snapshot of where you are now in each of these areas.

In-depth Meanings

While it is possible to do useful and accurate readings based on what you already know, you may desire a deeper meaning of the cards. After all, there are lots of symbols incorporated in the images as well as other ways to look at the cards. The method of developing in-depth interpretations described here will work for anyone, but be aware that this is not something you can do in an afternoon or spare evening. Depending on how much time you devote to your studies, it can take several months. Go slowly and enjoy the journey. You don't have to master everything all at once for the tarot to be useful.

For this method, you'll need at the very least one page of paper for each card. More than likely you'll use more. A three-ring binder could prove useful, as you can add pages as needed while keeping all your notes on specific cards together. For each card, write the name of the card at the top of a sheet of paper.. Then you can begin adding any notes, observations, and experiences you have with cards. The notes from the exercises above are an excellent starting point. Start your notebook by writing down your initial observations and feelings about the cards. If any of the cards remind you of situations, events, or people in your own life, add them as well.

Your own impressions are a strong beginning; you are already forming your own relationship with the cards. You can add to your own experience and base of knowledge by drawing on the wisdom of tarot experts, people who have devoted much time and study to the tarot. See the recommended reading list for some suggestions. There are also many resources available on the Internet. You can find websites with interpretations, spreads, tips, and techniques. You can also find and join chat groups devoted to tarot where you can ask questions and share ideas.

Once you have gathered some reference material (and just one book on interpretation is enough to get you started), pick a card that you want to work on. Read all the material you have available on the card, noting in particular things that ring true, that catch your interest, or that don't seem to make sense. Write all these things in your notebook. Once you've gathered as much information as you can, read it though and then set it aside. Think about it for a day or two. Then pull out your notes and some fresh paper. Spend time trying to condense all the ideas into a coherent essay. If you have any questions that are still unanswered about symbolism or meanings, write them out on a separate sheet of paper so you can follow up later. Go through your essay and highlight the major points. Use the major points to form a paragraph. Finally, select a single keyword that will trigger your memory and help you recall the paragraph. This is the secret to using keywords—the keyword is derived from your larger interpretation and acts as a gateway so that you can easily access all the details you've learned about the card. As you learn more or find answers to some of the questions you wrote down, you can modify your essay and paragraph and even your keyword as needed. This method may take effort and time, but it works very well.

Readings

You've learned a lot already—enough, in fact, that you are ready to do a reading. In this section you'll learn everything you need to know to do just that, and you'll read some examples, as well. Whether you read the cards for yourself or someone else, remember to relax and enjoy the process.

reading for yourself

Reading for yourself is one of the most useful and interesting uses of the tarot. Most people are familiar with having
someone else read your cards. While that can be fun and
helpful, reading for yourself allows you more control over
the information you seek by customizing your spread to
your needs and by practicing clarification techniques as
needed. In addition, you can spend time with the cards,
sometimes seeing more in them than the meanings given
by a reader. There are challenges involved in reading for
yourself, though. Being objective in your interpretations
can be problematic, especially if you want the cards to
favor a specific outcome or decision. Your own desires may
cloud your judgment or make being honest with yourself
troublesome. Overcoming these issues takes discipline and
practice. It is worth it.

reading for others

Reading for family and friends can be an effective and fun
way of developing your skills. Just a few caveats, though.
Until you feel confident, make sure they understand that
you are still learning your art. You may get stuck on a card
or may want to consult a book while reading. It is fun, as
well, to read for and with someone else who is also learning
the tarot. Getting insights and perspectives from others can
greatly aid your own learning. Also, keep in mind while
reading for others that your own biases should not affect
your interpretations. If you've just been treated badly by a

significant other, don't let that influence your readings about relationships for others. And don't let the tarot be a vehicle for expressing what you want for your friend. You may think that quitting her job and leaving for three months in Europe is a bad idea, but it may be just what she needs to do. Read what the cards say, not what you want them to say.

performing a reading

Once you've formed your question, selected your spread, made your decisions about significators and reversals, and you have some level of confidence about how to interpret the cards, you are more than ready to start reading. You will need to mix the cards by shuffling any way that is comfortable for you or by laying them on the table and mixing them like you're making mud pies or playing in finger paint. Focus on your question as you mix the cards. When you are ready, put the cards in a neat pile and either lay the cards out one by one from the top of the deck or fan them out facedown and select each card.

Lay each card out in the order indicated by the spread. You can lay them facedown (with the back of the card facing you) or faceup (with the front of the card facing you). There are benefits to both methods. If they are facedown and you flip them over (along the card's vertical axis, as you would turn a book page) one at a time, it increases the sense of mystery and excitement and also allows you to focus more easily on one card at a time. By laying the cards faceup, you get an opportunity to see the spread as a whole before beginning to read each card. This can be helpful in determining the theme of the answer. Many Major Arcana cards, for instance, might indicate a very spiritual bent; many Cups would show a very emotional situation; several Aces would indicate a time of beginnings. Sometimes symbols or colors can speak to the answer as well. Let's say you laid three cards to represent one choice and three more to represent another; if one side were very dark in color and symbology and the other very light and optimistic, that could indicate that one choice is more positive than the other.

Once you've laid out the cards, you may begin interpreting them, keeping in mind what position each card is in, as position affects the interpretation. Once you've finished, you might want to record your reading in a journal or notebook. This is highly recommended. By doing this, you can see if certain cards keep appearing in your readings. Also, you can go back to your readings and check your accuracy of interpreting the spread and your objectivity. Hindsight is always twenty-twenty. Even if your objectivity isn't all that you'd hope at the moment, you can improve it. By reviewing your readings and seeing how what you wanted affected your interpretation, you'll be better prepared to guard against this sort of influence in the future.

chapter two

Rituals

So now you have the tools you need to perform divinations. Maybe the process isn't as theatrical or mysterious as you expected. Maybe you wanted a little more drama. Although little extras certainly aren't always needed, they don't hurt. In fact, they can be helpful. Rituals help focus the mind, and items that carry significance for you can provide useful, positive energy. Here a just a few ideas you might want to experiment with.

- Create a space for your reading by setting the mood. Burn candles and/or incense selected to promote concentration, communication, or union with the divine. Have physical representations of the suits nearby to as reminder to seek balance in your readings. A candle or twig for Wands (Fire), a chalice or glass of water for Cups (Water), a small knife or feather or incense for Swords (Air), and a stone or bit of soil for Pentacles (Earth).

- Prepare yourself by centering and grounding yourself. Take a few deeps breaths, pray, or mediate before shuffling.

- Create a ritual for shuffling your deck. Many readers choose to shuffle seven times, both because seven is a mystical number and because it randomizes the deck very well. Some people like to cut the deck in three piles and then gather them up in random order before dealing the cards.

- At the end of the reading, store your deck for the next time. Some people "cleanse" their decks after each reading by putting all of the cards upright, arranging them in a specified order, or smudging them. Other ideas for storage include wrapping the cards in silk or putting them in a wooden box, sometimes including crystals or stones with divinatory or other desirable properties. If you wrap your deck in a large enough cloth, you can use the cloth on the table to lay your cards on. One hint here: don't select a busy or overly colorful cloth, as it might compete visually with the images on the cards—the images should be your main focus.

Now that you have all the tools you need to do a reading, you might find an example helpful. In this example, you'll see how Leslie phrases her question, interprets the cards, and comes to a conclusion.

Tom and Leslie

Although the tarot can be used for any sort of question, most people ask about either relationships or finances. In this reading, Leslie seeks guidance about her relationship with Tom, whom she has been dating for two years.

Leslie wants a more committed relationship; put simply, she is ready to get married and start a family. Tom does not feel he is ready to make that commitment. Leslie feels frustrated and doesn't know if she wants to invest any more in the relationship if it is not moving toward marriage.

She phrases her question like this: "What are the ramifications of staying in the relationship as opposed to ending the relationship because it isn't quite what I want?" She decides to use a simple seven-card spread, with one card in the center representing the crux of her indecision and three cards on each side representing the issues involved in either decision. Using the *World Spirit Tarot,* she draws the following cards.

Crux of the matter: Six of Cups

Staying with the relationship:

Seven of Pentacles

Sibyl of Cups (Queen of Cups)

Sage of Cups (King of Cups)

Ending the relationship:

The Sun

Temperance

Four of Wands

A quick overview of the cards indicates that the situation is highly charged emotionally—not surprising in a relationship spread. The court cards on the "staying with the relationship" side show that various personalties are involved—also not surprising. The only Major Arcana cards are on the "ending the relationship" side, indicating larger issues in Leslie's life.

The Six of Cups shows two people in garden. The image of this happy couple sharing a comfortable, con-

tented moment reminds Leslie of her childhood, which was a happy one. She remembers her parents being very much in love and focused on enjoying their children and home. Because the suit is Cups, Leslie knows that the card speaks to her emotions rather her mind. It could be that her heart has romanticized her memories. Whether accurate or not, this notion of family life is one that she seeks for herself, and she is frustrated because Tom does not share the same goal.

Leslie finds the next three cards interesting because there are two court cards and one pip card. She decides, then, that one court card represents herself and one represents Tom. So it makes sense to her to read the pip card, the Seven of Pentacles, as an overview of the issues overshadowing her question about staying in the relationship. Pentacles (or Coins) represent tangible things, resources, or things created. A relationship takes work and nurturing and can be seen as something cre-

ated, something that requires resources in the form of time and emotional investment. The Seven of Pentacles is a card of looking at the work done, the investment made, and considering whether you are pleased with the results. Leslie feels that she has worked hard for two years and is not happy with the results. She wants something more for the efforts she has put forth.

There are several ways to read court cards, but, as said above, Leslie has decided to read the Sibyl (Queen) and the Sage (King) of Cups as representing herself and Tom respectively. This is a relationship reading. Since it concerns two people, it makes sense that the court cards are read as the people involved in the question. Such a choice is part of the art of tarot reading; if there are multiple possible meanings, the reader must decide which one is most pertinent to the reading.

The Sibyl of Cups indicates a person very comfortable with emotions and interested in nurturing the emotions of others. Clearly, this is what Leslie wishes to do. In contrast to Leslie, the Sage of Cups, representing Tom, is quite the opposite. Although the cards are from the same suit, the Sage is shown surrounded by swirling emotions yet sitting above them, untouched and slightly uncomfortable.

The cards on the left give an accurate picture of where things stand for Leslie. They also give her a clue about Tom. He is uncomfortable with delving deeper

into his emotions and exploring a more committed relationship at this time. This is not to say that Tom will never want to get married and have children; he may have issues that will take time to work out. The Seven of Pentacles reminds Leslie to consider the work already invested and to decide if she wants to continue to cultivate the relationship.

On the the other side, the cards representing ending the relationship paint a more ambiguous picture, which makes sense, as that situation is less defined in Leslie's mind. Be-

19 THE SUN

cause she loves Tom and doesn't really want to end the relationship, she has not spent much time imagining what life would be like without him. The Sun shows a happy child enjoying the warmth of the sun and surrounded by flowers. This somewhat mirrors the Six of Cups, and Leslie thinks she may rediscover her optimism regarding her relationship goals if she seeks a new partner. Because the child is alone in the card (as opposed to two figures shown in the Six of Cups), she begins to wonder if she hasn't been neglecting her self-development.

Temperance, a powerful and beautiful angel pouring liquid between two chalices, shows the ultimate in balance and grace. Leslie realizes that she has been putting quite a bit of energy into the relationship and, consequently, not addressing enough attention to other aspects of her life. Perhaps by separating from Tom, she can achieve more balance.

The Four of Wands is a card of celebration and many read it as the "marriage" card. Leslie cannot know for sure that it means certain marriage, but she does know that whatever form it takes that this card indicates celebration of some sort.

Leslie decides to have a heart-to-heart discussion with Tom. Perhaps they can discuss why he is uncomfortable with a deeper emotional attachment and plan how they can work together to move toward a common goal. If not, Leslie decides that since her needs are not being met and have no immediate hope of being met, she must move on. It crosses her mind that Tom may need time alone to sort things out and that meanwhile she can work at developing other areas of her life.

The cards did not tell Leslie what to do. Instead, they illustrated the situation and gave her information to consider in the process of making her own decision. Her conscious mind was unaware of Tom's issues with emotions. Now that she understands she may be able to achieve her goals by showing patience and understanding while discussing this with Tom. On the other hand, she also learned that her life has been unbalanced for quite some time due to her intense attention to the relationship. Although this reading was a lot more work, and ultimately entailed more responsibility, than simply asking, "Should I leave Tom?" the results give Leslie more control over her life as well as illuminating facets she had not before fully considered.

This sort of divination takes a bit a practice and much self-reflection, but it is indeed one of the most common uses for the tarot.

While all divination is, in a sense, a form of problem solving, there are other techniques for specific problem-solving situations. We will explore these in the next chapter.

Chapter Three

Problem Solving

One of the ways that the tarot "works" is by tapping into your subconscious, rather like the Rorschach inkblots sometimes used by therapists. Looking at an image and focusing on what draws your attention or causes a reaction can help pinpoint or clarify issues on your mind—issues that, while apparently clamoring for attention, might be difficult to see clearly. Also, considering the actions depicted in the cards can provide inspiration for new ideas or new ways of looking at situations. This makes the tarot very useful for problem solving.

Reading the Images

In her book *Tarot: Your Everyday Guide*, Janina Renée describes a method that is particularly suited to problem solving. In addition, it is well suited for beginners. Ms. Renée suggests reading the pictures—that is, looking carefully at what is going on in the scenes and adapting those actions to the situation at hand. By focusing on the scenes, a beginner can use the cards without extensive study. In some cases, knowing too much about the esoteric meanings can actually hinder this method, as readers may be tempted to focus on their interpretations of the cards rather than the specific actions pictured. Sometimes extreme familiarity with a deck can stop a reader from seeing the cards with fresh eyes. If you find that is the case, you might consider using a deck with which you are unfamiliar to force yourself to examine the cards more carefully.

The method is very simple and works well with a one-card spread. Consider your problem. Shuffle the deck, asking the tarot for advice on how to handle the situation. Draw a single card, look carefully at the picture, and determine how the action depicted can be applied to your situation. Keep in mind, this method entails far more than merely aping the actions shown on the card. This exercise is about tapping into the energy and power contained in the image and translating into your own life.

Here are a few one-card illustrations of this method addressing very specific problems and everyday issues.

Julie

Julie has a very busy job and doesn't enjoy engaging in a lot of chitchat at the office. However, one coworker, Tina, very much enjoys chatting with fellow workers. Julie, although reasonably assertive, is having a difficult time disengaging herself from her talkative coworker. She pulls a card from her *Nigel Jackson Tarot* deck, asking for a direct action she can take to deal gently yet effectively with this situation. She pulls the Eight of Coins, showing a man busy at work, weighing out coins and writing notes. Everything about the man in the card suggests a sort of nose-to-the-grindstone concentration and focus. His body language communicates his focus and his desire to not be interrupted. Julie realizes that she can use this card as a model. When Tina comes around or stops Julie in the hallway, Julie need only adopt similar body language and point out that she is quite busy and focused and isn't able to visit. Although the solution seems obvious and simple, Julie feels more confident that she will be better prepared to deal with Tina in the future by tapping into the energy represented by the Eight of Coins. She might even carry the card or some object to remind her of the card in her pocket as a sort of talisman, a tangible reminder of the energy portrayed in this card.

EIGHT OF COINS

Steve

Steve is up for his annual review at his job. He's been with the company for two years and feels he has accomplished quite a bit and has taken on much more responsibility; consequently, he thinks he is due a substantial increase in salary. However, he is aware that the company is not doing as well as expected. The problem: how to best present his case for more money to a company experiencing budget constrictions. From his *Universal Tarot* deck, Steve pulls the Eight of Wands. Since this card shows no human figures, just eight wands flying through the air in a tightly organized formation, Steve is a bit at a loss. As he looks at the wands, he realizes that they are indeed specifically organized, moving quickly, and aimed at a specific goal. He decides to play down the company's current situation in terms of profit and instead focus on where the company is going. He thinks of projects that he has worked on that are near completion and that promise much success. He studies trends and is able to provide sound analysis about where the company is headed and his role it. Thus empowered, Steve feels more confident about his salary request and is able to prepare a rational presentation.

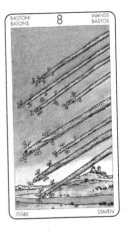

Susan

Susan, a single woman, is taking a class on French cooking through a local store. The class is nearing its final weeks. In addition to enjoying herself, she has met several new friends who share a common hobby. In particular, she is interested in a man who seems as shy as she is. She'd like to ask him out, but isn't sure how to approach him. Her  problem: how do two incredibly shy people connect? She is surprised when she draws the Seer of Wands (Page of Wands) from her *World Spirit Tarot* deck. The woman on the card, all fire and determination, fearless as she pets a large cheetah, seems the very opposite of herself. She meditates on the figure, trying to find that aspect of herself. Feeling just a bit silly, she stands, adopting the pose of the Seer—feet spread, feeling grounded and balanced, her face determined and confident. After getting used to the pose, Susan finds she is able to tap into her own boldness. Susan can almost feel the cheetah next to her and as she, in her mind, pets this powerful creature, she feels its confidence and boldness fill her. She practices feeling comfortable with this attitude so that she can slip into easily when she next sees her classmate.

While the above examples illustrate how to use one card to find solutions to specific or immediate problems, some problems are more complex or you may simply want a more detailed course of action. The following example applies this method to full reading.

Tess

Tess is feeling rather in limbo about her small craft business. Busy purchasing and moving into a house, she has not invested much energy into her business for several months. Further, her sister and soon-to-be partner, Kathy, who currently lives out of state, is in the process of moving closer to Tess in order to facilitate business operations. It will be several more months, though, until Kathy relocates and they move forward with their business. Her problem, Tess feels, is how does she reconcile what is immediately occurring in her life with goals for her business. She feels guilty about the lack of attention she is giving her business and wonders what she should or could be doing to attend to her business during this down time.

Using the *Celtic Dragon Tarot* deck and a simple three-card spread described in Janina Renée's *Tarot: Your Everyday Guide*, Tess lays the cards for her reading. The first card is the action card and the other two are supporting cards.

The first card, the focal card, representing the main course of action, is the Two of Cups. This is supported by the Ten of Pentacles and the Knight of Cups.

Two of Cups

Ten of Pentacles

Knight of Cups

First, we look at the general meanings based on the information we learned in chapters 1 and 2. There are two Cups, which represent emotions. The lack of Wands (inspiration or endeavors) or Swords (intellect or problem solving) is interesting because we would expect to utilize those energies in developing a business plan. Instead, we can see that Tess has emotional issues to attend to at the moment.

Tess focuses on what the characters in the card are doing. In the Two of Cups, two figures hold a single cup while a dragon fills the cup from his own. This, Tess feels, indicates the upcoming business partnership between herself and Kathy. The dragon represents a source of spiritual guidance and elemental power indicated by the suit of Cups—they are forming an emotional and creative bond. The act of working together will create an environment conducive to receiving inspiration. Even while still separated by distance, Tess and Kathy can spend time talking and writing about their ideas. Without the immediate need to focus on production, marketing, and bookkeeping, they can indeed draw from the element of Cups—nurturing creative ideas and long-term visions for their future.

The Ten of Pentacles shows a couple walking into a castle. Tess feels that this card suggests that she should use this time to focus on settling into her new home and on her relationship with her husband.

The Knight of Cups shows a young knight riding forth, but rather than looking straight ahead, he is enjoying the surrounding sites. A girl's face, representing another aspect of the knight, looks off in a different direction. Only the two dragons are looking straight ahead. Tess believes that during this time she will find her correct business path by not focusing on the outcome. Rather, if she slows down, daydreams, and follows her fancy, she will, in time, discover an unexpected plan.

While the reading really reinforced what Tess wanted to do, it also helped her realize that although she may appear idle in terms of her business, in the long run, she was actually doing more to strengthen both her business and her relationships. By waiting for her sister to move, Tess ensures that the business will be shaped by both her and Kathy and will reflect the unique alchemy created by their relationship. By focusing on her home and family during this time, Tess strengthens that bond which (as she knows) gets stretched during the fall and winter seasons. Finally, taking time to dream and be quiet allows Tess to hear the voice of

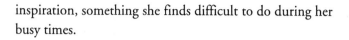
inspiration, something she finds difficult to do during her busy times.

Reading for Two

The examples above are ways individuals can solve problems. Many times problems exist between two people. If both people involved are willing to use the tarot as a tool, there are methods they can use to facilitate discussion with a goal of solving problems. For example, sometimes people have a hard time discussing certain topics, either because they are uncomfortable with the topic itself or uncertain about how to express their feelings. One method would be for each person to select a card that represents how he or she feels in the situation and to form a dialogue as if between the two cards rather than the people themselves. This can create enough distance to help both people feel safe and to help both visualize the other person's point of view.

Tom and Leslie

Let's revisit Leslie and Tom's situation from chapter 2. At this point, Leslie has asked Tom for a heart-to-heart discussion about the future of their relationship. Tom is, as he has said before, "just not ready for a commitment." Leslie asks if he'll try to talk about the situation by looking at her cards and picking one that represents how he feels. Although unfamiliar with the tarot, Tom is willing. He does love her, after all, and does not want her to leave. They agree that the problem they will focus on is how to achieve a compromise between Leslie's desire for marriage and children and Tom's desire to keep the relationship as it is. They go through Leslie's *World Spirit Tarot* deck, selecting one card to represent how they feel about the other's goal for the relationship. Leslie quickly and easily selected the Five of Cups, showing a woman kneeling on the ground, mourning, as five cups turned topsy-turvy spill their liquid. Tom takes longer, but finally he selects the Four of Pentacles. Leslie notes that neither picked The Lovers, so she pulls it out as a sort of focal point.

FIVE OF CUPS   6 THE LOVERS   FOUR OF PENTACLES

First, they both take a few minutes writing as the character in their cards and share what they have written with each other. Tom writes of feeling like he only has so much time, money, and resources and that family life would take too much away from him. Like the man in the card, he feels the need to hold tight to what he values in order not to lose anything. Leslie writes about all the effort she has invested in the relationship and how heartbroken she feels because everything she's hoped for is beyond her grasp and all her efforts wasted. Then they begin talking, trying to understand the other character, asking questions. She asks about him seeing the women and children at the well—doesn't he want that to be part of his life? He asks why she feels so badly about the spilled cups.

The discussion is long and productive. They both have a much better understanding of themselves and each other. They both agree that the discussion may not have taken place as it did without using the cards. However, they are no closer to a compromise or any sort of decision. Both are steadfast in their initial decisions. In desperation, Leslie pulls a card, simply asking the universe for some sort of guidance. She pulls The Hermit. The solitary figure following his own path, seeking his own inner truth, is not what either of them wanted, but they agree that a short separation might be the best solution in this situation. It would give them time to reflect on the conversation undistracted by the every day aspects of their relationship.

Achieving a Goal

Part of Leslie and Tom's problem was having no agreed-upon goal. Some problems, though, are that there is goal, but you just don't know how to achieve it. The tarot can be useful here as well. For this technique, you can either read the images, as described above, or you can read them as you normally would (assuming you have developed your own meanings). First, go through your deck and select a card that illustrates the current situation. Then, go through the deck again and select a card that represents your goal. For the next step, you need to make a judgment call regarding the number of cards you pull for the steps between your present situation and your goal. If you are taking on a large or complicated challenge, you may wish to pull four or five cards; for a smaller challenge, one or two cards might be sufficient. If you are unsure, drawing three cards is usually good starting point.

Achieving Your Goal Spread

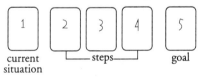

current
situation

steps

goal

Laura

Laura, a thirty-something career woman happy with her life, has been haunted by the idea of taking a summer off from her well-ordered life and traveling the Far East. With her job, her relationship with her boyfriend, her cat, her condominium, and her financial responsibilities, she cannot imagine how this would ever be a possibility without losing what she has worked so hard to achieve. Just because "it couldn't hurt," Laura decides to see if the tarot has any suggestions. Using the *Universal Tarot* deck, Laura selects the Nine of Pentacles to show her current situation—a woman who has created a wonderful life for herself through her own efforts. The Fool, she decides, most represents her goal of a long, grand adventure in Asia, unencumbered by any other responsibilities. She lays the cards out, the Nine of Pentacles to the left and The Fool to the right, leaving enough space between for three more cards. (See spread illustration on facing page.)

The three cards she draws are the Three of Wands, The High Priestess, and The Hanged Man.

The Three of Wands, with a person standing in a castle looking at ships out at sea, seems like an obvious first step to Laura. For her, this card shows someone dreaming of travel, of the first moments when the desire becomes stronger, more demanding.

The High Priestess puzzled her, though. How does hidden, mystical knowledge apply? Laura uncomfortably realizes that The High Priestess might be asking her why she wants this trip, whether there is something deeper driving this desire. It could represent the ability to research the scheme and come up with realistic figures for what she'd need both to travel and to maintain her home while away. Actually, Laura has not even taken the time to research the real costs of such a trip. The financial aspect seemed so overwhelming and impossible that she just looked on her desire as a sort of pipe dream. Perhaps The High Priestess is hinting that there is much that Laura doesn't know about the possibilities, that there are options, and all she need do is look for them.

The Hanged Man makes her nervous—she has heard that he represents a sacrifice of some sort. Laura looks closely at the picture, trying to feel The Hanged Man's experience. She notes the radiance around his head. It makes her think of sudden realization. She imagines that after making the sacrifice he realized something that he couldn't before. In this card, the actual sacrifice turns him upside down. Maybe being upside down has given him a new point of view, allowing him to see something in a different way. She realizes that until she completes step two, determining the costs, she cannot move to the final step of understanding the full extent of the sacrifice. Indeed the sacrifice might be that she must alter her ideal trip in order to go at all.

After consulting the tarot, Laura has a sketchy game plan. She will begin researching options and crunching numbers while examining why she wants this experience.

Talk Amongst Yourselves

In Laura's case, her problem was how to achieve a specific goal, something she very much desired—or at least thought she desired. Sometimes our problem is that we are avoiding something we absolutely don't want to do. In many instances problems or confrontations can be dealt with through careful, rational communication. The trouble is that we often approach difficult conversations fearfully or defensively, which only adds to an already emotionally charged situation. Often when we participate in a challenging conversation, we are thinking only of our point of view and our feelings. By doing this, we are not doing everything possible to achieve our ultimate goal—whether it is getting our way or facilitating compromise. We saw how Leslie and Tom used the tarot to help them with a conversation. But many times it is not appropriate or possible to use that technique. In those cases, how can the tarot help?

One key is to think about the other person. What is his or her position? What are his or her needs? What types of arguments or reasoning would appeal to him or her? Consider these questions as objectively and honestly as you can. Meanwhile, pull all of the court cards from your tarot deck. Go through them carefully and pick one that you think represents the other person in this situation. Then select a court card that depicts you in this situation. Imagine a dialogue between the two court cards. Where is there a conflict? Where is there a meeting of the minds? Is there any way the character in the card representing you can approach the other card in a positive way? Try imagining the other court cards talking to the other person. Which ones are more successful? Can you adapt any of those characteristics? Here are a few examples of this technique in action.

Brian and Judy

Brian and Judy are a young married couple, fairly well established in their careers, living in an apartment in the busy city where they both work. They have managed their finances very well and have a respectable amount of money saved. Judy would like them to buy a house. She is tired of paying rent year after year and having nothing to show for it. Parking is always a nightmare. At this point in her life, she'd like something a bit more stable and convenient, in addition to making a real investment with their money. Brian, on the other hand, loves living in the city, enjoys their busy social life, and takes advantage of all the activities the city has to offer. Whenever Judy brings up the idea of buying a house, Brian refuses to consider the idea. Judy gets angry, Brian gets defensive, and nothing is resolved.

Judy considers the court cards from the *Universal Tarot* deck. She easily selects the Knight of Wands for Brian—all energy and activity, never sitting still, never wanting to be tied down. She picks out the Queen of Pentacles for

herself—carefully managing resources, trying to make a comfortable and attractive life, and looking ahead further than the upcoming weekend.

Just seeing the cards next to each other, Judy can see the conflict. The Queen of Pentacles would go on and on about the stuff: the house itself and all the benefits (garage, basement, laundry room). The Knight of Wands would complain about the responsibility: the upkeep, the lawn care. Their priorities are too different.

Is there any hope for compromise? How can two so vastly different sets of priorities find peace together in one household? Judy thinks about the court cards and their qualities. Which card can mediate between the Queen of Practicality and the Knight of Activity? Either the King or Queen of Swords, with their keen intellects and superior problem-solving skills, could work. But Judy and Brian are fairly emotionally invested in this and the King might be a little too brusque. The Queen of Swords could probably handle the problem with more compassion.

Judy considers the issue from the point of view from the Queen of Swords. She tries to embody and channel the energy and personality of the Queen and to distance herself from her own emotions. She sees one person, Brian, who is perfectly content with the way things are. She sees another who is mostly happy but has some core issues that she thinks will be answered by the purchase of a house.

She lists these core issues:

1. Putting their money to good use

2. Having convenient parking

3. Having laundry facilities in the home

While Brian does agree with Judy's points, he does not want a house because of the responsibility, specifically lawn care. He also does not want to be far from the city. Is there a way, then, that Judy's concerns can be addressed without the yard work and distance from the city? Judy finds it interesting to think of this problem as if she were an outsider. It is helping her to see things from Brian's point of view without getting defensive. And breaking down the problem, just as the Queen of Swords would, helps her realize that buying a house isn't the issue as long as her concerns are addressed. In fact, she is amazed at how simple the solution seems. Although, when she considers their previous conversations—fraught with defensiveness, as they were—she can see how they missed it. A condominium in the city would suit both their needs perfectly and would be an acceptable solution.

Actively searching for solutions, doing exercises, and thinking about things from another person's point of view are all excellent ways to solve problems. Some solutions are very elusive, though, and will not be drawn out by active searching. In fact, active searching can even make solutions even more elusive. Sometimes you just need to shut up, close your eyes, and listen. In a word: meditate.

Meditation

Meditation has long been recognized by many cultures and religions as a beneficial practice. For all meditation's acknowledged benefits, though, the idea of sitting quietly for an extended period of time is often not immediately appealing or practical for some people. Lives are busy, and if we have a spare half-hour, there is surely something that needs to be done. But busy lives need balance, too. And all too often our inner lives are what we neglect the most. Meditation can restore the balance.

Meditation is more than just zoning out for a while; it is useful and practical. Through meditation we can find our calm center, create a space of inner peace, and re-energize our minds. While meditating, we can find answers that seem to elude our fast-moving conscious minds. We may find the inspiration we've been seeking. Like the tarot, meditation is a tool that can be adapted to your needs.

There are many different types of meditation. Two will be discussed here. Both practices include focusing on a specific object—in this case, a tarot card. One is guided meditation, where the meditation is carefully scripted. The other is self-directed, where the outcome is not scripted. There is another type of meditation often connected with tarot cards called Pathworking. This is associated with studies of the Kabbala and the Tree of Life. The Major Arcana cards correspond to the paths that connect the spheres on the Tree of Life. It is a specific type of mediation designed to trigger archetypal responses. This is a powerful course of study that requires discipline and knowledge. The benefits, though, can change your life. To learn more, see the Suggested Reading list (page 175).

The benefits of meditating with the tarot are twofold. First, it provides a way to learn the cards themselves, and, second, it allows access to your higher self. By quieting the mind of its internal chatter and focusing on one specific symbol or image, you can access knowledge and peace that eludes you in your busy day-to-day life.

Meditation is not all that mysterious or difficult. But because our lives are so hectic and so filled with activity and sound (even if just our own thoughts), being quiet and focused can seem mysterious. And, if truth be told, it can be difficult at first. Our minds are so used to racing that slowing down can take practice. But with practice, it does get easier. For those who are inexperienced with meditating or find meditating difficult, guided meditations may work better. Guided meditations are often taped ahead of time (all sorts of tapes or CDs are available or you can make your own) or read aloud by another person. By having something to listen to and by being directed to visualize things, the mind always has something to guide it.

On the other hand, to meditate on a single card on your own—self-directed meditation—takes a bit more discipline. But it has its own benefits as well. While listening to a guided meditation, the creator of the meditation has more control over the path your thoughts travel. By meditating under your own direction, you can explore whatever you feel would be most helpful to you at that moment.

Whichever form you practice, you will want to follow some similar procedures. First, you'll want to make sure you have a safe, comfortable place where you won't be interrupted. You may wish to burn incense conducive to meditation (refer to Dorothy Morrison's *Everyday Magic* for ideas). You'll want either to sit straight, with your feet flat on the ground or lie down on your back with your spine straight. You may wish to pray for guidance from a higher power or invite the presence of spiritual powers you are accustomed to working with. A short relaxation technique may be helpful. Start at your feet and consciously flex and then relax your toes, your soles, your ankles, and so on up your body. Even with the body relaxed, many people forget to relax their jaw muscles, so you will want to make sure you check that. You'd be surprised how much tension is held there. Calm your mind and take three long, slow, deep breaths. At this point, you should be ready for your meditation, whether guided or self-directed.

Guided Meditation

For guided meditations, there are several excellent books available. One is Stephen Sterling's *Tarot Awareness*. It provides shorter guided visualizations for the twenty-two Major Arcana. After you become more familiar with cards, you may wish to write your own. Writing your own meditations can be a valuable part of the process of learning both meditation and the cards. It can be particularly helpful if you feel blocked about a card and have questions about it. Your meditation can take the form of an interview with the card in question. Because you are in a very relaxed state during meditation, you should have an easier rapport with your subconscious and answers may come more easily.

Guided meditations are very useful, both to learn more about the cards and, specifically, more about yourself in relation to the cards. It is true that most tarot meditations are about the Major Arcana. This is in part because the Majors are more archetypal, more spiritual, and deal more with larger issues and concepts than the Minors. It is also because we think of meditation as a spiritual practice, one that helps us along our spiritual journey. The twenty-two cards of Major Arcana are often viewed as a journey that each of us follows through our life and our own spiritual development. The Fool, either unnumbered or numbered as zero, is the starting point—we are a fool, ready to start on our journey through life or a particular phase in life. We then journey through life, where all of our experiences are illustrated by the Major cards. Our parents show up in

The Empress and The Emperor, our adolescent arrogance in The Chariot, our need to "find" ourselves in The Hermit, our realization of the need to sacrifice for a greater goal in The Hanged Man, and our optimism and hope in the face of troubling times in The Star. Each of the Major Arcana represents an important step in spiritual growth. We'll discuss these steps more fully in chapter 7.

Self-Directed Meditation

Self-directed meditation, especially when combined with journaling (discussed in the next chapter), can be a wonderful way to learn the cards themselves and about your journey. It is also a way to learn not only about the energy and power of a card, but to help you discover ways of using that energy and power in your life.

To begin a self-directed meditation, select the card you wish to explore. Examine the card; memorize the details of the image until you can close your eyes and still picture it. Prepare yourself for meditation as described above. After you are relaxed and ready, picture the card itself. When you have the card fixed in your mind, let it change from a picture to an actual scene or landscape. When you are ready, visualize yourself entering the scene. Does someone speak to you? What does he or she say? How do you respond? Do you have any questions for the characters there? What are the answers? Do they surprise you? How do you feel in the scene—safe, frightened, uncomfortable, angry, joyful? Do you want to join the activities or are you hesitant? Your reactions can tell you a lot about how you feel about certain types of energy, attitudes, or situations. Here is one example.

Leslie

Remember Leslie—our friend who is taking a break from her relationship with Tom? Since then, she has been drawing a card a day, to help her learn about the cards and for daily guidance. On one particularly challenging day, she draws the Wheel of Fortune from her *Nigel Jackson Tarot* deck. This is one card that she particularly dislikes, especially now, since she feels her life, specifically her relationship with Tom, is entirely out of her control—that someone or something is spinning a roulette wheel and she has no

X THE WHEEL OF FORTUNE

idea what will be the outcome. Looking at the card—the blindfolded woman impassively measuring out lengths of thread, the wheel dispassionately spinning, not seeming to care about the figures grasping, trying to hang on as their situations constantly change, and the figures themselves, passionately trying to hold on—Leslie wishes she could get the woman to remove her blindfold, to show some concern. It just seems wrong that life could spin with no concern about those affected and hurt. She would like to give Fortuna, the goddess of fate, a piece of her mind.

Leslie has heard about self-directed meditations with tarot cards and decides it couldn't hurt to try now. At the very least, she'll be able to vent at the implacable goddess blithely ruining her life. She lights some lemongrass incense, sits comfortably in a chair, and focuses on the card, memorizing every detail. She calms herself and relaxes her body. Enough of her anger and frustration wane so that she can murmur a sincere prayer asking for guidance and wisdom. She closes her eyes, picturing an open field and sky filled almost entirely with white clouds. In the sky, she sees a large wheel with four figures attached and a larger-than-life woman, half obscured by the clouds, spinning thread on a spindle attached to the wheel. As Leslie approaches the scene, the wheel drops lower in the sky and miraculously stops spinning. The woman—all right, there was no denying it—the goddess sets down her spindle and removes her blindfold. With those cold, penetrating eyes boring into her, Leslie's resolve melts. Fortuna, with a hint of impatience, shocks Leslie by saying, "I understand you have words for me."

The conversation that follows is less than comfortable for Leslie. However, it is productive. She is reminded that life is about cycles and that everything that happens is for her own development. Fortuna points out that Leslie is supposed to be exploring The Hermit—finding herself and strengthening her own inner peace. In short, that to achieve spiritual growth, she needs to focus less on the wheel and more on the axle. If she becomes the center, if she herself were stable and centered, then the rest of life will not destroy her. One of the figures on the wheel, being a human and understanding that the human condition is not always so simple (something that goddesses might forget from time to time), takes pity on Leslie. He points out that whatever goes up, must come down and vice versa. He suggests that, concerning her relationship with Tom, she is probably at the bottom and that things will improve from there. Either they will come to an agreement or the pain will end and the wounds begin to heal.

Leslie finishes her meditation with much to think about. Even though she doesn't get to vent at Fortuna and go on about the unfairness of life, she does get something. She remembers that she may not control every aspect of her life, but she can control how she behaves in the face of it. She also finds some comfort that things are bound to improve one way or the other, sooner or later. In the meantime, she will focus on her inner peace.

Meditation offers a quiet way to access your higher wisdom. Often, after meditating, journaling is a helpful way to sort through, track, and incorporate what you've learned. In addition, journaling provides its own connection with the divine. It is journaling we will discuss next.

———————————————————⭐

Journaling

Most any beginner book on tarot will suggest keeping a journal—and with good reason. Nearly every tarot activity is enhanced by the use of a journal. It is helpful for documenting your readings, recording your ideas about the cards, noting insights gained during meditation, and practicing various exercises using the cards. And, as Francis Bacon said, "Writing maketh an exact man." The very act of writing urges us to sort out our thoughts, to draw parallels, and to notice patterns. If we view our study of tarot as a spiritual journey, our journals become a sort of travelogue of our lives.

Just as with many activities, journaling can be as simple or complex as you wish. You can simply keep a legal pad handy and jot down your ideas and readings in a chronological fashion. If you pull one card a day for study and inspiration, you can note the daily card on your calendar. You can purchase an expensive, beautifully bound journal and an elegant pen for your activities. You can have a variety of journals, pens, markers, colored pencils, rubber stamps, or whatever strikes your fancy. Many students of tarot find that using two separate journals works well. If you use a three-ring loose-leaf binder for your notes on studying the cards, then you can organize it so that each card has its own section and adding pages is easy. If you also have a large artist's sketch pad, you will have room to draw your spreads with room for notes and observations. You can go back to readings you've done in the past and use a different color pen to add notes about your initial interpretation and how the situation unfolded. The large, blank pages will also allow room for creativity and uninhibited exploration with the exercises suggested in this chapter.

In addition to the materials needed, there are varying opinions about how often you should write. The best answer is whenever it works for you. You may wish to write everyday. You may write quite a lot if you are going through a rough time or are intensely focused on your study of the tarot. You may go days or weeks without writing.

Where you write can also make a difference. Some people like to have a special spot for their journaling. Others will write wherever the mood strikes. You might want to keep a small notebook and pen handy to jot down random thoughts or observations that you can later transfer to your larger journal. However you choose to use it, the journal is a tool; it's there to help you, not stifle you.

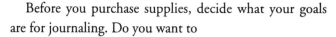
Before you purchase supplies, decide what your goals are for journaling. Do you want to

- write about a card per day?
- record your readings?
- do various exercises?
- keep notes on each card?
- detail your spiritual journey?

Think about what you hope to accomplish, your habits, and your preferences. Two caveats: if you think a very expensive, elegant journal will intimidate or inhibit you, don't use it. It is important that you feel free to write what you want and not be nervous about making "mistakes" or writing neatly. Also, journals that don't lie flat when open can become frustrating to write in. Adapt the ideas and exercises that follow to suit your needs. Above all, enjoy your journey.

Journaling Exercises: Working with a Single Card

One of the most basic journaling exercises is to draw a card from the deck every day. There are several methods for selecting the card. If you are new to tarot and want to learn each card, you can start with The Fool and work sequentially through the Major Arcana and the Minor Arcana. If you are becoming comfortable with your overall grasp of the cards, then you may want to focus on specific cards, selecting ones that are problematic for you or that seem to have relevance to your life at the moment. You may also want to let chance take over and just draw a card. Drawing a card at random from the deck serves a twofold purpose: it provides a card to work with, and it gives a little message from the universe, rather like a daily horoscope. Here are a few exercises to help you begin journaling.

describe it

Sometimes one of the most challenging aspects of journaling is getting started. This exercise is a simple way to start writing and to become intimately familiar with the images on the cards. Select your card and simply describe it in as much detail as you possibly can. Don't analyze it or interpret—just write what you see.

challenge your memory

This exercise is helpful as preparation for self-guided meditation on a particular card. It will help you be able to bring the card to mind easily and will also help you identify any issues, ideas, or questions you may have about the card. Select a card and examine it closely for a minute or two. Memorize every detail, every symbol, all the colors. Set the card aside and write for five minutes in your journal. Begin by describing the card in as much detail as you can. Continue writing about the card, noting the symbols that resonate with you or puzzle you. After five minutes, compare your description to the card itself. What did you miss? What stood out the most? What would you like to know more about? What revelations surprised you? After this exercise, you may want to try a self-guided meditation on the card, using your notes to shape your adventure.

daily message

After you've done the preceding exercise, keep that card and your observations in mind throughout the day. See how many different ways the card—its meanings or its symbols—show up in your day-to-day routine. At the end of the day, record your experiences. Did the card offer any advice that helped you? If you drew a court card, did you or any of the people you encountered exhibit any of the traits of that card?

free writing

Free writing is an easy and sometimes surprising activity. Select a card and just start writing for a predetermined amount of time (five minutes works well, but if you're on a roll, there is no need to stop when time runs out). Write anything that pops into your mind, even if it seems to have nothing to do with the card in front of you.

walk in its shoes

Select a card and identify the main character. Imagine that you are that character. What are you doing, wearing, holding? How does it feel? What is the environment like (weather, landscape)? Is it comfortable or disconcerting?

Are there other figures there? What do you say to them? What do they say to you? If someone entered the scene, seeking wisdom, what would you tell him or her?

letter writing

If you are having trouble understanding a card or find that a card keeps coming up in your readings and you just don't understand why, this exercise is particularly helpful. Think about the card and your questions, then write a letter to the card or the character in the card. Reread your letter and then write a response as if you were the recipient. You can get as creative as you like with this activity. Try writing your letter as yourself, using whatever medium you normally use—e-mail, fancy stationary, a card, a piece of lined paper. When you write the response, use what medium you imagine the character would use—parchment-style paper, a legal document, a fancy marker, disappearing ink, crayon, whatever.

Theresa

This correspondence between Theresa and the Ten of Pentacles (*Universal Tarot* deck) is a good example of the letter-writing exercise.

To the Lady of the Pentacles
My lady,
　　You and your lovely family have been showing up in my readings

very consistently for some months. Can you tell me why? Being uprooted, nearly a thousand miles from my family and friends, living in a small apartment with my new husband, working all the time to make ends meet, being thousands of dollars in debt, and seeing my life passing quickly before my eyes, I have a hard time with you and yours taunting me in my readings. Any light you can shed will be much appreciated.

Yours respectfully,
Theresa

Dear Theresa,

My family and I are very blessed. Throughout the years we have managed our resources, made mistakes, suffered setbacks, but we have always practiced the art of gratitude. If you look closely at your life, you will see that although distance separates you and many of your loved ones, you still enjoy strong, loving relationships with them and are building a strong marriage with your new husband. You do work a lot, but you have work that you enjoy (and remember that no job is perfect). Look also at how far you've come in achieving your financial goals. Your home— if not exactly your dream house—is certainly a sanctuary where you and your husband are comfortable and can enjoy your pursuits. We are trying to tell you that the Ten of Pentacles is a state of both actuality and perception. Practice seeing your life in terms of

what you have, not what you think you want, while
moving ahead toward your goals.

> Count your blessings,
> The Lady of the Pentacles

one on one

Pick a character from the card you've selected. Describe the
character—what she looks like, what she is wearing, her
mannerisms and personality, her relationship to you. What
do you like or dislike about her? How is she similar or different from you? What aspects of her would you like to incorporate into your own life? What aspects appall you?
Why? Does she remind you of someone you know? How
do you feel about that person and what is your relationship
with that person like?

Leslie

We last left Leslie after her conversation with the characters in the Wheel of Fortune card. Her goal, which the
goddess Fortuna reminded her about, is to find herself, to
develop her own calm center. It has been several weeks
since she and Tom spoke. They have an appointment to
get together in two weeks to discuss the future of their relationship. Leslie has not been idle and wants to do a sort
of reality check to clarify where she is in terms of developing herself. She pulls a card at random from her *World
Spirit Tarot* deck: the Three of Pentacles. There are two
characters in the card, one presenting samples for the

other's approval. Leslie focuses on the woman presenting the sample work. Leslie writes:

"This woman, an artist, is in her studio, surrounded by her work. She stands confidently holding up her book of samples. She doesn't seem a bit apprehensive about showing her work, doesn't seem to care whether the other person is impressed or pleased with her work. Indeed, she seems utterly unimpressed with him—his rich garments, his ability to provide her with high-paying work, his opinion, none of that fazes her. She seems almost absurdly arrogant. Why isn't she appealing to him, working harder to convince him to choose her and her work? Isn't she afraid he will reject her? What do I like about her? Well, she is clearly talented and productive. It seems like she has accomplished a lot. But she isn't seeking recognition or validation from someone who is obviously in a position to provide it. What don't I like? That attitude—that 'here's what I am, take it or leave it' thing. Gggrrrr. Why don't I like it? Right. Because in two weeks, I'm going to be laying out my 'work,' what I've accomplished in the past month. I'm going to be looking for Tom's approval. I going to want him to be pleased and impressed. I'm going to want him to 'buy' my work, to approve of me. To not reject me.

Evidently I've still not got it right; I'm not focusing on me yet. How can I become more like Ms. Take-me-or-leave-me-I-don't-give-a-damn?"

Now that Leslie has a pretty clear picture of her current challenge, she might consider doing another exercise to help her become the person she wants to be. If you were Leslie, what would you try?

location check

Go through your tarot deck and find a card that represents the phase you are in your life. This card can depict where you are in your life as a whole or a specific aspect: physical, emotional, or spiritual. How do you feel about the card? What do you like or dislike? What would you change? Is there anything in the card that would help you make that change? If there is a particular aspect that you'd like to focus on changing, follow up by selecting a card that shows that change. What do you need to do to accomplish that change?

make your own cards

While few of us feel artistic enough or dedicated enough to create our own full deck, the following exercise can be extremely useful and enlightening. Committing yourself to designing a full deck is intimidating; instead, pick a single card that you are interested in exploring—whether it is a troublesome card or one that you want to realize more fully in your life. Use collage, markers, paint, fabric, found objects, or any other medium you like. Think of symbols, quotations, poems, and colors that you associate with the card. Be creative—you are not obligated to make it card-sized or even two-dimensional. Keep it in your journal or hang it up for inspiration. After a period of time, it can be illuminating to make the same card again, noting how your vision of the card has changed.

Journaling Exercises: Working with Multiple Cards

Working with one card at a time is a great way to learn the individual cards and develop both your own relationship and your own interpretations for them. Working with multiple cards allows you to learn the cards' relationships to each other, and doing so also allows for more complex explorations.

storytelling

Storytelling is an excellent why to practice weaving the cards together into a coherent whole—an important skill when interpreting a spread. Tarot cards are often compared to an unbound book, with each card presenting a new character or scene. Shuffle your deck and lay out three cards. Starting with the first card, begin to tell a story, with as much detail as you like. Move on to the next, incorporating the image into your narrative. Wrap up your story with the final card.

Tarot cards have also been compared to panels in a comic strip or graphic novel. Lay out three or more cards. Photocopy or sketch them onto a piece of paper and create a graphic story, using conversation balloons, short narrative remarks, and any embellishments you'd like.

For a more complicated story, select cards specifically for the main characters, the setting, the plot, the climax, and the resolution.

These ideas can be fun as a party game or as a group exercise if you and your friends are studying the tarot together. Use one deck and have each person draw a card. Someone begins a story using his or her card. The next person continues the story, incorporating the card he or she selected and so on.

Sometimes adults have trouble with storytelling—their imaginations may be rusty or they may feel too much pressure to "get it right." Working these exercises with children can be inspirational and surprising.

dreams

People who are familiar with working with their dreams often use journaling for recording and interpreting them. Dreams can be enlightening. They can also be confusing. While dreams and tarot cards have much in common—both have symbols and provide a connection between our conscious and subconscious minds—there is a distinct difference. Tarot cards, unlike, dreams have assigned meanings (whether they are meanings you have developed or ones you use from a book), and so they can provide a sort

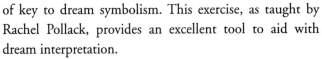

of key to dream symbolism. This exercise, as taught by Rachel Pollack, provides an excellent tool to aid with dream interpretation.

Write down your dream in as much detail as possible. Then go through and write the dream as a numbered list of discrete elements from your dream. Using the list as a guide for a spread, shuffle your deck and lay out the same number of cards as there are elements in your list. Use the cards to help interpret each part of your dream.

Beth

Beth used this exercise to interpret one of her dreams.

1. In a grocery store

2. I am about seven years old

3. With little sister in a cart (about four years old)

4. Mother is with us; she seems scattered, ineffectual

5. Father is in the store but not with us—we are scared of him

6. Convinced mother to take us to aisle where there is "special" oatmeal

7. As we passed the end caps of each aisle, my sister and I screeched (chillingly and loudly), not sure why—to scare or confuse father?

8. The floor suddenly covered with mice and toads; we were very afraid

Using the *Nigel Jackson Tarot* deck, Beth pulled the following cards:

1. **Page of Staves (Page of Wands):**
   Pages represent new beginnings, courses of study, someone who is a novice. Beth recently separated from her husband, so she sees the grocery store as an exciting place full of new things. She can now fill her cart with anything she likes.

PAGE OF STAVES

2. **Seven of Swords:** Because seven shows up twice, it is evidently an important number in this dream. Beth thinks of The Fool's Journey, which is usually laid out with The Fool at the top and the remaining twenty-one Major Arcana arranged in three rows of seven cards each. The card shows a fox, usually associated with being sly or clever. Swords represent challenges. She has had to be more clever than usual to reach this point in her life and isn't comfortable with that.

SEVEN OF SWORDS

TWO OF COINS

3. **Two of Coins:** This is a card of balance. Although she had to be clever, bold, and secretive to make a break from her husband and reach this point in her life, she still has her "little sister" or her guileless inner child to help her stay balanced.

4. **Nine of Staves (Nine of Wands):**

NINE OF STAVES

This card, showing a sturdy castle, well fortified against attack, is in direct contrast to the mother figure. Beth feels like her ability to do mom-type things (take care of herself, make decisions, protect her inner child) is not well developed at this time. Some facet of herself is not doing its job and it scares her.

5. **The World:** The father figure, like the mother figure, scares Beth. This dream figure represents the world—everything, all of the opportunities, all of the choices, all of the unknowns that Beth is facing for the first time in many years. The mother and father are not functioning together.

6. **Death:** Oatmeal, something somewhat bland and yet also comforting, plain and simple, nourishing, and definitely not scary. If Death represents an end, then by seeking out the bland and familiar oatmeal from the many choices available at the store, Beth attempts to put an end to the frightening feelings induced by the huge array of selection in the grocery store.

SEVEN OF CUPS

7. **Seven of Cups:** The card represents fantasies that may be delightful to contemplate, yet can distract one from one's goals. By screeching and giving voice to her fears, Beth distracts herself from the task of facing them and incorporating them into her life.

8. **Judgement:** The Judgement card asks us to hear a higher calling, to think outside our little boxes. The mice and toads represent the many little ways Beth is being called to rediscover and recreate herself. The calls are not dangerous, but they seem too many to handle, to organize, to deal with all at once.

XX JUDGEMENT

Beth realizes now that she is faced with many challenges at once. While exciting and promising, they feel overwhelming. Furthermore, she feels ill-prepared to deal with them. She feels like a child who is being asked to do more than she is able. The parts of her that she would normally draw on are unavailable or not behaving properly. Beth decides to work on her ideas of mother and father roles, how those roles are currently expressed in her life, and how she can develop those skills in such a way that they work together and help her navigate her new life without fear. She starts a special section in her journal to devote to The Emperor and Empress.

Journaling works well with practically all uses of tarot. It helps focus and consolidate your thoughts and chart your progress. Somehow writing things down makes them seem more real. In that sense journaling is a type of magic. There is other magic, though for which the tarot can be used.

Magic

Magic. What images come to mind when you think of magic? Do you believe in magic? Do you practice magic? What is magic? The answer to that last question depends largely on whom you ask. A very simple definition is that magic is the art of using your will to achieve changes in the world. Beyond that, there are lots of methods, ideas, opinions, debates about ethics, etc., involved with magic, but focusing the will is a good place to start. This chapter will discuss the very basic and most simple types of magic. You are encouraged to read some of the wonderful books available on magic. Janina Renée's *Tarot Spells*, Christine Jette's *Tarot for All Seasons*, and Dorothy Morrison's *Everyday Tarot Magic* are excellent starting points. All of these books focus on using tarot as part of your magical workings.

Technically, the tarot practices described thus far in this book are types of magic. Divination, by focusing your will, intending to connect with the divine, and asking for wisdom, is certainly a form of magic. You use your will to change the world; you receive knowledge that you did not have before you performed the reading. What follows will help you broaden and enhance your tarot magic.

Intention and Responsibility

Intent is extremely important in any magic and, indeed, in any use of tarot cards. For the cards to be effective, you have to want their wisdom, you have to be open to whatever comes, and you have to be intent on finding answers. So it is with magic. You have to intend for whatever you are doing to work. As with prayer, meditation, or therapy or counseling, you have to have faith in the process.

Magic also brings with it a sense of power. With that power comes responsibility. Don't just think through what you want to do but also *why* you want to do it. Just as many tarot readers will not do a reading about someone without his or her consent, many people who practice magic will not do anything that meddles in another person's life. In the Wiccan religion, those who practice magic are familiar with the threefold law—that is, whatever you do for good or ill will come back to you threefold. Most other faiths have a similar precept. The laws of karma say that your present and past actions affect your future.

Christianity tells us that you will reap what you sow and to do unto others only what you'd have them do unto you. Magical practitioners often say, "Do what ye will and harm none." In any case, recognize your power and be mindful of your responsibility.

Now that you have been sufficiently warned, be assured that magic is not necessarily a big, scary complex thing. We are actually raised with a sort of magic. Most of us know the rhyme "Star light, star bright, first star I see tonight, I wish I may, I wish I might, have the wish I wish tonight." The star provides a focus for our will, for our energy and speaking the words shows our intent. Most families have birthday cakes for children. Parents tell children to "make a wish and blow out the candles." Different families have different traditions, such as if you tell your wish, it won't come true or however many times it takes to blow the candles out, that is how many years before the wish comes true. Although most people probably don't believe that either of these practices actually work, they are examples of magic. (Remember, though, for magic to work, you do have to believe.)

Because magic is based on focusing your intent, most magic involves rituals and/or accouterments of some sort to facilitate this intense focus. The ritual can be as simple as lighting a candle (or blowing one out). Or they can be long and complex, thoroughly researched and designed within the parameters of your own spiritual practice and full of esoteric tools and props. We'll discuss here some basic elements of ritual and provide a very loose outline for preparing, performing, and following up a magical act that you can adapt for your own use. There are plenty of books of spells and rituals out there, but do feel free to adapt and change spells you come across or even create your own. Sometimes the most powerful magic you can perform is changing yourself, so make your magic your own.

Getting Started

The first step—deciding what you really want to do—is sometimes the most difficult. Start by identifying what you are unsatisfied with in your life. That is usually fairly simple. Now the more challenging part: what would make it better? For example, are you unhappy at work? Do you and your boss not get along? Do you think your job would be better if she weren't in the picture? Do you really want her to lose her position? Or would you rather develop a better relationship with her? Or maybe it's time for you to seek a new position. The former solution may seem easier, but is it the best solution? What are the ramifications? Ethical considerations aside, how do you know a new boss wouldn't be worse? Think of another example, one from your personal life. Are you lonely and wishing there was someone to share your life with? Tempted to cast a spell making the attractive man down the block fall for you? Or would the outcome be better if you focused on preparing yourself for love to enter your life? Deciding on the best course of action is often no easy matter.

To help you decide how best to change a less than satisfactory situation, you may want to do a reading, a meditation, or a journaling exercise to help you get to the root of the matter. Although this part may not seem as fun, interesting, or exciting as designing and performing the magical ritual, this groundwork is necessary for your success and happiness. If you have identified the thing you wish to change and then manner in which you intend to change it, you may want to do the following divination to help you consider some of the ramifications. Go through your tarot deck and select two cards, one to represent the situation as it stands and one to illustrate how you intend to change it. Lay those two cards down side by side. Go through your deck again, selecting a card that shows what you intend the outcome to be. Leave that card in your deck and shuffle the deck, focusing on your intentions. Draw three cards and lay them out vertically to the right of the first two cards. These cards represent outcomes of the spell. Is the card you selected to represent your desired outcome among them? Are the cards promising or disturbing? Consider what they are telling you. If you are satisfied with the outcomes, then proceed. If not, try to imagine other ways to achieve your goal.

Spell Spread

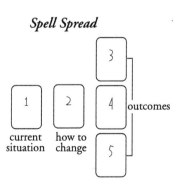

If you've any doubts about what you are doing, you may wish to employ this ending prayer, which I learned from a wonderful author and friend, Christine Jette. Say (and mean) something like: "Let this be or something better, for the good of all and harming none." It is a kind of two-way escape hatch. It gives room for the universe to provide something better than what you asked for, but it also allows the universe to ignore your plea if it would harm someone else.

Designing Rituals

Once you've decided on what you hope to accomplish, write it out as clearly as possible in your journal. You'll want to record the experience from beginning to end so that you can analyze the success of your ritual. Now you are ready to design your ritual. This is the basic framework for performing a simple ritual.

1. Cleanse yourself and space. Some people actually take a ritual bath. You can do that or simply calm your mind and take three deep, cleansing breaths. The space you are working in should be neat and provide enough room to set up your tools or focus objects. You might consider smudging the area with sage to banish unwanted energies.

2. Set up your altar or focus objects.

3. Call any spirits or elements that you work with or want to work with. If you follow a Pagan or

Wiccan path, you could cast your circle at this time. (If you want to know more about casting a circle, see *The Elements of Ritual* by Deborah Lipp.)

4. Perform your ritual action. This is the heart of the ritual and can be as simple or complex as you like, depending on your experience and preferences. The basic elements used here are selecting a card that represents the current situation, a card that represents the desired outcome, inviting that energy into the situation, and visualizing the successful outcome. A candle, a tarot card, or any meaningful object can be used as a focal point during visualization.

5. Thank the spirits or elements; thank the divine; open the circle if you cast one.

6. Clean up your area (if applicable).

7. Record the experience in your journal.

Before getting into details of more elaborate rituals, let's take a look at a simple ritual that incorporates the first six steps yet only takes a few minutes.

Gina

Gina works in a medium-sized office, full of the usual office politics, cliques, and gossip. She often finds the atmosphere catty and herself participating in unkind gossip. She doesn't like this about herself and seeks to change the behavior. By refraining from any conversation, she'd feel antisocial and as if she were only addressing half of the problem. She not only wants to stop saying hurtful things, but she also wishes to encourage kindness in others. She wants to perform a spell that will help her avoid gossiping and instead become more of a peacemaker.

Gina follows the framework outlined above to design her ritual.

1. *Cleanse yourself and space.* Gina clears off her dresser and takes three cleansing breaths.

2. *Set up your altar or focus objects.* She sets out a pink candle for friendship and harmony. She selects the Five of Staves (Five of Wands) and the Two of Swords from her *Nigel Jackson Tarot* deck, setting the Five of Staves upright, the Two of Swords facedown. The Five of Staves shows a very combative situation. The Two of Swords shows two warriors agreeing to a truce.

3. *Call any spirits or elements that you work with or want to work with.* Gina doesn't practice a particular religion and so calls, in a moment of silent prayerfulness, on the general spirit of the universe to aid her cause.

4. *Perform your ritual action.* Picking up the Five of Staves, Gina says, "Spirit of contention and gossip, I banish you from my mind and my words." She lays the card on the dresser facedown. Picking up the Two of Swords, she says, "Spirit of friendliness, peace, and harmony, I ask you to guide my thoughts and my words." Gina places the card faceup on top of the Five of Staves. She lights the pink candle, gazes at the flame for a few moments, focusing on feelings of peace and harmony.

5. *Thank the spirits or elements; thank the divine; open the circle if you cast one.* Gina thanks the universe for hearing her prayer and for helping her be an instrument of peace and kindness.

6. *Clean up your area (if applicable).* Gina decides to leave the cards on her dresser for a few days, so she can be reminded of her intent before she goes to work. She blows out the pink candle.

In her journal, Gina notes the date and her intentions. She then describes her ritual and the words she spoke. In the days to come, she will record the office mood and her part in it, noting how it has changed and how she feels the spell worked.

tools and props

Gina's example shows just how simple a tarot spell can be. She used two cards and a candle as focal points and a few simple words were enough to help her achieve the desired change in her life. Magic users have many other tools at their disposal, though. Here is list of some items that you might want to use in your own work:

Incense: Incense in general can set a meditative or spiritual mood. Different scents also have different properties that can enhance your spell work. For example, sandalwood and sage help with protection, lemongrass with psychic ability, and lavender and rosemary with love.

Stones, crystals, and gems: Many people use crystals or stones in their magical workings. You can perform a ritual where you charge a crystal with energy and carry it with you as a sort of a talisman to remind you of your goal. You can, for example, use rose quartz for love, tiger-eye for protection, and amethyst for courage.

Candles: Candles, like incense go a long way in setting a meditative or mystical mood. Spell workers use different color candles for different purposes: for instance, green for prosperity, red for courage, blue for clarity. White candles are used for spiritual guidance and are considered an all-purpose candle, appropriate for most situations.

Tarot cards: As depictions of power archetypes, the Major Arcana cards are particularly suited for magic. Select a card that embodies characteristics you'd like to incorporate into your own life or your spell work. Consider The High Priestess for wisdom, The Empress for abundance, or the Wheel of Fortune for change.

You may also wish to include representations of one or more of the elements in your ritual.

Fire (inspiration, career or projects, spiritual guidance): a candle, the Ace of Wands, or a small twig.

Water (creativity or emotional issues): a cup of water, the Ace of Cups, or a chalice.

Air (challenges or clarity of thought): incense, the Ace of Swords, or a small knife or dagger.

Earth (manifestation, grounding, or physical issues): a small amount of salt or earth, a stone, or the Ace of Pentacles.

The suggestions above are very basic and simple. To give your magic more focus, you can research a variety of other factors and learn additional techniques that can affect your ritual. For instance, the different phases of the moon, or even what sign the moon is in, can affect the energies you are working with. If you are comfortable working with a variety of deities, you can read about different ones and their associations. You can work alone or with a friend or group. You can follow up with daily affirmations and/or meditations. The combinations are endless. Experiment and discover what works for you.

Whatever you choose to do, remember that the power to change your life is within you. Seek the highest good and be honest with yourself. Sometimes being honest with ourselves is not as easy as you'd think, though. Sometimes we need to channel our energy more specifically in order to create change in the world or, as is often the case, to create change in ourselves. Now we'll look at ways that we improve ourselves.

Self-Improvement

Doing divination, meditation, journaling, or magical work are all ways of improving yourself. The exercises and ideas given in this chapter do not fall neatly under any of those categories, but they are all ways of using the tarot to improve your life, mainly by gaining a better understanding of yourself.

Almost everyone knows his or her astrological sun sign. Knowing your sun sign can give you a quick snapshot of some of your main characteristics, potentials, and challenges. These first two exercises will give you something like a sun sign. Most people interested in astrology also know that their sun sign is just one component to their astrological makeup. To get a more accurate picture, you would have your natal chart calculated and interpreted. The last exercise is more complex—more like a natal chart—and will therefore yield more information.

Life Card Exercise

Many of those who believe in reincarnation believe that in each lifetime we have certain lessons to learn. Whether you believe in reincarnation or not, many believe that we are born in this life with a purpose or lesson to learn as well as strengths to develop and challenges to overcome. This first exercise, based on numerology, will help you identify your Life Card. For this exercise you will use the Major Arcana only.

Write out your birthday in numerals. Add up the numbers. Add the individual numbers of that sum until you have a number that is less than twenty one.

For example, if you were born on November 21, 1975, you would begin by adding

$$11 + 21 + 1975 = 2007$$

then add the individual numerals of 2007

$$2 + 0 + 0 + 7 = 9$$

which is under twenty-one. Now see which Major Arcana card is numbered nine. In this case, your card would be The Hermit. You are probably something of a loner, wise before your years, confident but quiet. Your challenge may be to reach out to others.

Let's try a person born on February 7, 1963. You would add

$$2 + 7 + 1963 = 1972$$

and then

$$1 + 9 + 7 + 2 = 19$$

which is under twenty-one. However, you can still add

$$1 + 9 = 10$$

In cases where the number is under twenty-one but over nine, you will have two Life Cards. This person would have The Sun and the Wheel of Fortune. What do you think would characterize this person and his or her life?

Tom and Leslie

Let's go back to Leslie and Tom and see if their Life Cards can shed some light on their lives and relationship.

Leslie was born on January 7, 1976.

$$1 + 7 + 1976 = 1984$$
$$1 + 9 + 8 + 4 = 22$$
$$2 + 2 = 4$$

Leslie's Life Card is The Emperor. She values stability and a well-ordered life. She takes pride in and is good at organizing things, be it a company or a family. Her challenges include being a bit rigid and possibly too authoritative.

Tom was born December 13, 1975.

$$12 + 13 + 1975 = 2000$$
$$2 + 0 + 0 + 0 = 2$$

Tom's Life Card is The High Priestess. He knows things but keeps them to himself. He probably enjoys being self-contained, pretty much whole unto himself. His challenge would be to communicate his feelings clearly and openly.

Looking at this pair of cards and these interpretations, it is fairly easy to see where conflict would arise. These are both strong cards and both individuals feel they know the best course of action. However, Leslie would be more extroverted and active in realizing that course. Tom, on the other hand, would be more passive and may feel that Leslie is trying to "run the show" without consideration for his needs. It might help them if Leslie could let go of her ideas of how things "should be" and find ways to encourage Tom to share his ideas. Tom could work on developing plans to realize his desires and communicating with Leslie.

Year Card Exercise

Just as we may have a large theme for our life, we also have smaller cycles within our lifetime. Each year often seems to have a theme. Just as we calculated a Life Card, we can calculate a card for the year. It is done the same way as a Life Card, except that you substitute the current year, or the year you are curious about, for the birth year.

Tom and Leslie

Tom and Leslie are having a particularly challenging year in terms of their relationship. Let's see what the tarot can tell us.

Leslie's Year Card calculation would look like this:

$$1 + 7 + 2002 = 2010$$
$$2 + 0 + 1 + 0 = 3$$

Leslie's Year Card is The Empress, which is incredibly interesting because The Empress can represent motherhood. In this case, it is probably safe to assume that this is the year her biological clock is starting to tick. She has wanted a family her entire life, but this year the desire is demanding to be addressed.

Tom's Year Card calculation would look like this:

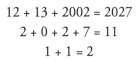

$$12 + 13 + 2002 = 2027$$
$$2 + 0 + 2 + 7 = 11$$
$$1 + 1 = 2$$

Tom has two cards for this year: Justice and, again, The High Priestess. This seems to be a year when, as the saying goes, the chickens come home to roost. Tom is reaping what he has sown, getting his karmic payback for good or ill. And, as The High Priestess indicates, he knows it. What is it that Tom is reaping? What has he sown? These are questions only he can answer. But he isn't telling, which makes the situation between him and Leslie even more difficult.

The Fool's Journey

Your Life Card and your Year Card provide a small part of the overall picture of your life. As you would no doubt agree, your life is quite complicated. How can you get a more detailed picture? For just such a purpose, tarot expert Rachel Pollack has devised an exercise called the Alternative Major Arcana, an amazingly useful spread based on The Fool's Journey. But before we can learn this exercise, we need to understand what we mean by The Fool's Journey.

Many tarot experts and enthusiasts view the twenty-two Major Arcana as an accurate depiction of a journey through life, a journey of self-development and spiritual growth. We all start as The Fool, the first card of the Major Arcana, though all our journeys are different.

One way to visualize The Fool's Journey is to spread the cards, placing The Fool alone at the top, then laying out the rest of the cards in order underneath The Fool in three rows of seven (as below). The Fool, the traveler who stops at all the other Major Arcana, represents each of us. At these points along the journey, The Fool gains experience and knowledge associated with the other cards. The first row shows the steps we go through in our basic development from birth to young adult. The second row illustrates the universal laws or rules of society that we must confront, question, and come to terms with. The final row is our spiritual development.

The Fool's Journey

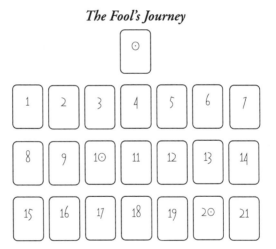

0. **Fool:** The Fool marks the beginning of the journey, as an archetypal child, unformed and unlearned, innocent and eager.

1. **The Magician:** The Magician represents the male principal or animus. These are our active or outgoing energies, our skills and abilities in terms of the external world.

2. **The High Priestess:** The High Priestess embodies the female principal or anima. These include our passive or introspective energies, our skills as they relate to our inner world and self-reflection.

3. **The Empress:** The Empress represents the mother archetype and our experience with mothering, nurturing, emotions. This card also represents our creative impulse.

4. **The Emperor:** The Emperor represents the father archetype and our experience with authority, reason, and logic.

5. **The Hierophant:** The Hierophant is our formal education within our society, including school, religious training, and cultural traditions.

6. **The Lovers:** In a word, adolescence, our experience of hormones, sex, and our sense of self.

7. **The Chariot:** The Chariot illustrates the ability to see both sides of issues; it marks the ending of the "but that's not fair!" stage.

Once we have dealt with these archetypes with some degree of success, we are usually deemed fit to participate in society. Some of us may deal with the archetypes more successfully than others. In some cases, we may barely be holding our own. For example, if you know someone who "has issues with her mother," she may not have dealt very effectively with The Empress.

The next part of the journey concerns finding balance in the world and society.

8. **Strength:** Strength is where we learn to control our instincts and impulses, where we master ourselves and develop self-control. We may want to party all night, eat the entire buffet, or shop until our credit card reaches its limit, but we realize that it is probably best if we do not indulge all these desires.

9. **The Hermit:** The Hermit often plays out in people who feel the need to "find" themselves. We turn inward, questioning all we've learned, and try to find a sense of inner peace.

10. **Wheel of Fortune:** Just when we feel at home with The Hermit and are starting to feel centered and balanced, our resolve is tested by a spin of fate. Something happens beyond our control or our ability to foresee.

11. **Justice:** In the aftermath of the spin of the wheel, we find out how we fared and realize that we reap what we sow. If we were well prepared, we come out perhaps shaken but okay. If not, we may need

to revisit The Hermit phase of the journey—or move on to . . .

12. **The Hanged Man:** The Hanged Man shows us the strength and power of letting go and enjoying the view from a different perspective. This card also shows us the importance of sacrifice. Some things are worth sacrificing for, and maybe we really can't have it all. At least not the way we planned.

13. **Death:** Just when we get comfortable hanging on by a thread, we are faced with a major change in our lives. This can be any major change, positive or negative, such as an unexpected promotion, the ending of a relationship, moving to a new place.

14. **Temperance:** After coming through a transforma-tional experience, we learn graceful balance and tolerance. We learn to adapt to changes in circum-stance while maintaining our center, our sense of self.

We have come through a very difficult phase of our de-velopment. We have faced Death in some guise. We've learned to maintain ourselves, to adapt to circumstances, not to rail against the seeming unfairness of the universe. What more could we possibly have to do? A great deal, ac-tually. We must address spiritual matters.

15. **The Devil:** Balanced, strong, and confident, now we are asked to confront our shadow selves, the dark aspects of ourselves that we fear and that may

control us in subtle ways. These may be aspects that, in confronting the Strength card, we learned to control or repress. This worked well for a while, but now we have the knowledge and experience not just to ignore and repress these aspects. Now we need to revisit them, learn to appreciate the positive qualities they can bring to our lives, and synthesize them appropriately.

16. **The Tower:** Although we feel we've got ourselves under reasonable control by now, the universe reminds us that we are not in control of everything. The Tower gives us a bolt from the blue that shakes our very foundation. This may differ from the Wheel or Death in that rather than disrupting the external circumstances of our lives, The Tower shakes the foundation of our belief system, which we have worked so hard to build.

17. **The Star:** The Star provides us guidance, hope, and optimism after cataclysmic events, giving us the strength we need to rebuild our crumbled foundation.

18. **The Moon:** While The Star guides us on our way, The Moon teaches us to question everything and to realize that things are not always what they seem. By the light of The Moon, we can lose our way or be distracted by enticing shadows. We can also have inspiring dreams. We must learn to tell the difference.

19. **The Sun:** After wandering in the light of The Moon, we emerge into The Sun with increased strength and self-awareness, with the certainty that we know ourselves, what we believe in, and what is real.

20. **Judgement:** The Judgement card calls us to a deeper spiritual realization. Often it is a call to action, to share your knowledge or experience with others.

21. **The World:** This is the end of the cycle. We have learned all of our lessons and have achieved integration, balance, and spiritual awareness.

Now that we've begun to understand the traditional journey through the Major Arcana, we can use this to develop an interesting and useful spread to gain deep insight into our own personal spiritual journey.

The Alternate Major Arcana Spread

This spread allows us more insight into aspects of the Major Arcana cards in terms of our own spiritual development. There are two approaches. The first is if you are uncertain about where you are and want the tarot to help you. In this case, you shuffle all the Major Arcana cards together to begin. The second approach is good if you already either have an idea of where you are at or if you are having trouble with a specific card. In this case, you select that card and leave it aside as you shuffle the rest.

After you've shuffled the cards, you lay the cards out just as illustrated for The Fool's Journey. If you've shuffled all the cards, the first card you draw will go where The Fool normally goes. If you've held one out, then that one takes the spot of The Fool. When all the cards are laid, you have before you is your Alternate Major Arcana spread.

To interpret this spread, you go row by row, starting, of course, with the top row. The first two cards lay out the basic issues for that row. The middle three cards are the work you must do, the issues you must face. The card right in the center of these three (in the center of the row, in fact) forms the test or crisis, while the cards on either side show what must be done. The last two cards are the achievements of that row. The sixth card is the direct experience you have after we accomplish the work of that line. The seventh card indicates what you can become. The second and third lines are interpreted exactly the same way. Just as The Fool's Journey moves to deeper levels of development, so it is with your Alternate Major Arcana.

This spread takes some time and patience, but the results are always worth the effort. Let's try an example.

Keri

Keri decides to let the tarot tell her where she is in her spiritual journey. She uses her *Universal Tarot* deck. The first card is The Tower, so Keri's Alternate Major Arcana spread is all about how she faces threats to her spiritual foundation.

Her first row is:

1. The Moon

2. The Emperor

3. Justice

4. Death

5. The Chariot

6. The Star

7. The Hanged Man

The issues for this row are The Moon and The Emperor, uncertainty and certainty. There is a tension here between what she cannot be sure of on an intellectual level, as illustrated by The Moon and its dark, shadowy energies, and the desire to order and make life secure, as illustrated by The Emperor.

The major test or challenge here is Death. This makes perfect sense, as The Tower and Death (and the Wheel of Fortune) are very similar. If her spiritual foundation is being shaken, she may feel something like a death—a transformation of what she believes. The two cards flanking this one, Justice and The Chariot, show the work she must do. In the case of Justice, she must reap what she has sown. If she has been lazy or dishonest with herself in terms of her beliefs, then she must face that. If she has built a good foundation that will serve her well, then her beliefs will stand the trial by fire. With The Chariot, she

must take active control. She must squarely face the damage with determination and will, not lamenting that it is "unfair." If she does this, then she will experience The Star, hope, optimism, and renewal. This will lead her to become The Hanged Man, someone able to let go with serenity, to sacrifice if necessary and know that everything will be okay. In short, she will synthesize the first two cards, the uncertain and the certain, and become a person of great faith.

Her second row is:

1. The Lovers

2. The Hermit

3. The Sun

4. Temperance

5. The Magician

6. The World

7. The Fool

Again, her row starts off with the tensions of opposites: The Lovers, representing union, and The Hermit, indicating a withdrawal.

The main test of this row is Temperance: how to maintain her center gracefully while adjusting to a changing environment. Keri must face The Sun, a card representing great happiness and contentment with where she is at. The Magician is concerned with Keri using her skills. These cards work well with Temperance, as The Sun shows her secure center while The Magician shows her using her skills to accomplish what she wants. Because The Lovers and The Hermit suggest a theme of relationship rather

than solitude, this row probably addresses her need to balance nurturing her own soul and reaching out to others. If she can achieve this balance, she will indeed have embodied the energies of the Temperance card. When she does this, she will experience The World, a complete fulfillment. Ironically, what she will become is The Fool, someone just beginning a new journey.

Her final row is:

1. The Hierophant
2. The Wheel of Fortune
3. Judgement
4. The Devil
5. Strength
6. The Empress
7. The High Priestess

Keri's final row looks less obvious, more complex than her first two rows. The main issues of this row involve traditional education or formal training (The Hierophant) and the uncontrollable fortunes of life (Wheel of Fortune). Because at the end of the last row, she became a new Fool, just beginning, it makes sense to assume that she will begin a new level of formal education but that her plans will be at the mercy of some unknown events.

Her main test is The Devil—temptation and bondage. It could be that the ups and downs occasioned by the Wheel of Fortune tempt her from her studies. The work that she must do in relation to her test are Judgement, thinking outside of the box and hearing a higher calling, and Strength, gently, lovingly, but firmly controlling her baser impulses.

When she does this, she will experience The Empress, a time of great creativity and nurturing of others. Her potential will be The High Priestess—a person of deep and mysterious knowledge.

Keri believes this spread indicates that the she is reaching the final phase of her current cycle: getting ready to become a Wiccan initiate. Her beliefs will be sorely tested and tried, but she will come out with incredible faith. Just when she thinks she has "arrived" and can rest awhile, though, she will begin a new level of study. Perhaps even the cards are being very literal here, and she may begin training to be a priestess of a coven.

While this spread is challenging, it is also superbly enlightening. Spiritual enlightenment doesn't just happen, after all, you have to want it, seek it. By doing this spread, you are in a way letting the universe know that you are not only open to but also actively seeking spiritual challenges so that you can continue to grow. This spread can let you know what is ahead and how you can prepare yourself to meet these spiritual tests. Make sure you write about your Alternate Major Arcana readings in your journal and note the tests and challenges as they unfold. Your journey is sure to be exciting. You'll want a record of it.

While learning about your spiritual journey and exploring the deepest realms of your subconscious mind are exciting pursuits, remember that what makes all this possible is quite small, made of paper, and must be purchased from an entirely corporeal retail establishment with quite worldly money. From the esoteric and heady realms of the spiritual, then, we will now explore the more mundane realm of tarot retailers and how to select the right tool for your needs.

Selecting a Deck

Learning about the tarot and all the ways it can work for you is exciting. Exploring the different ways to use the cards, to say nothing of the cards themselves, can seem bewildering, at first, but, hopefully, by now you see that you can easily create your own connection with the cards. There is another lesson left to learn, though; you are now faced with the prospect of acquiring your own deck. The sheer number of possibilities might seem like a double-edged sword. While we can be grateful that we have more than two decks to choose from, the hundreds of decks available may feel overwhelming. This chapter will help you make your choice.

Your First Decks

Although you will probably want to purchase a single deck to start with, many tarot enthusiasts will attest that one deck will not be enough to serve all your needs. The tarot is a tool, and, as the saying goes, things go easier when you have the right tool for the job. This chapter will help you decide which are the best tools for you. We will discuss what to look for in any deck and qualities to keep in mind while selecting a deck for specific purposes, and, finally, we'll end with an annotated list of decks and their specific characteristics.

In chapter 1, you learned the basic structure of a deck. You will want at deck with seventy-eight cards divided into the Major Arcana and the Minor Arcana, with the Minor Arcana being comprised of four suits each having cards numbered Ace through Ten and four court cards. As mentioned earlier, some decks associate Wands with the element of Fire and Swords with Air; some reverse this association. If you have a strong preference, make sure you choose a deck that matches your preference. Most beginners (as well as most advanced readers) prefer decks with illustrated Minor Arcana. The illustrations help serve as memory triggers while learning the card meanings. In addition, the illustrations provide the imagination with more range for activities other than divination.

The introduction of illustrations on the Minor Arcana is almost universally attributed to Pamela Colman Smith, who illustrated the Rider-Waite deck in the early twentieth century. Smith may have had inspiration from the nearly six-hundred-year-old Sola Busca tarot (available as *The Ancient Enlightened Tarot* from Lo Scarabeo). The Sola Busca deck, though, uses more obscure images, referring to biblical and Roman history, alchemy, and medieval philosophy. Smith's images are much more accessible and aesthetically pleasing than the Sola Busca images. Many books for beginners suggest that a student's first deck be the Rider-Waite deck. There is some sense in this suggestion, as many books use this deck to discuss symbolism and develop divinatory meanings. However, this deck does not appeal to everyone and contains images and symbols that may have been common ninety years ago but are less universally known now. Another option for a first deck could be one of the many decks that are illustrated in the Rider-Waite tradition but with a different style of art and symbolic language.

art and theme

The artistic style or theme of a deck is vital. Of course, you are more apt to use a deck that appeals to you aesthetically than one that you don't care for. You can narrow your possible choices by weeding out ones that just don't appeal to you visually. There is, though, more to a deck than its art. Many decks draw on different mythologies or spiritual practices for themes. If you are drawn to the art of a deck based on Arthurian legends but are not well grounded in the stories and characters and have no desire to learn them, then that deck may not be the one for you. Conversely, if you are very knowledgeable about Arthurian legend but don't like the art, then keep looking. If you are not knowledgeable but want to learn more, then a deck with a full-sized book may be the perfect choice.

size

Card size is another consideration. Many decks are a little larger than a pack of regular playing cards; some are significantly larger. Depending on your preferred shuffling method and the size of your hands, this may make a difference for you. While the larger cards may take a bit of getting used to in terms of shuffling, they have the advantage of larger art. Because many of us are drawn to tarot because of the art, this can be a deciding factor.

The Right Tool for the Job

Structure, artistic or thematic style, and card size are important in selecting a deck for any purpose. Different purposes will influence your decision as well. A deck that is great for divination may not be the best choice for meditation, journaling, or magic. Each job requires different tools.

For divination, a deck that has clear, easy-to-read images works well for most people. Think about the things you'll be looking for in a reading. When you have more than three cards in a spread, complex, intricate images may seem overwhelming. To help synthesize the cards into a coherent whole, you want to take in certain information at a glance, such as the suits and the numbers. Cards that clearly indicate the suit by either a different color border or display of suit element are useful. Very complex images are wonderful in that they often represent many facets of card meanings, but they may be too intricate to work well in larger spreads. Look for images that portray a clear meaning and that seem to interact with each other to tell a story. Cards with esoteric symbols can be incredibly useful if you are familiar with them. If not, keep in mind that you will have a longer learning curve as memorizing a new set of symbolism is like learning another language. Because your reading deck will probably be shuffled a lot, card size will be important. Also, consider the quality of card stock. Most decks published by larger publishers are made of a card stock that is sturdy while being thin enough to shuffle and that is coated so that they don't wear out too quickly. If you're considering a self-published or small-press deck, make sure the cards aren't too thick for easy shuffling or too delicate for constant use.

If you find that you are doing lots of readings for yourself and your friends, you may find yourself reading for certain types of information over and over. The most commonly requested readings are about love and money. You may want a certain deck for relationship readings or career-related readings. Having multiple decks for divination is less common than having different decks for other purposes. Most people find that their regular divination deck works just fine for a variety of readings. If, however, you are going to read for other people, you may want to be familiar and comfortable with different reading decks so you can offer your friends a choice.

Because meditation and journaling are different than divinatory readings, there are other considerations to keep in mind when selecting a deck. While clearer, simpler illustrations work better for readings, they may not be the best for deep exploration. Since you generally only use one card at a time for meditation or journaling, more complex, even ambiguous pictures will provide exciting and challenging places to visit. For readings, you are looking for a way to channel the subconscious to the conscious. For meditation or spiritual exploration you are looking for a doorway from the conscious into the subconscious. Look for images that invite you to enter another world. Larger-size cards that really showcase the art are excellent for this type of work. Since you won't be shuffling these cards as often, the difficulty or discomfort when shuffling associated with large cards won't be a factor, as it can be with a reading deck. Also, since this deck won't get the same sort of use as your reading deck, you could use a more delicate deck.

If you want a deck for magical and/or spiritual work and you follow a certain spiritual path, it makes sense to use a deck based on that belief system. In this case, the belief system may play a larger role than aesthetics. You may find it is more important to have the symbolism than to have pretty images to look at. For magical work, size will probably not be a deciding factor. Depending on what sort of magic you do (or on how careful or accident prone you may be), you may even consider laminating this deck to protect it from candle wax or water spills. However the tarot plays a role in your life, no one deck will be perfect for all uses; as with many things, it is a matter of priorities.

Shopping

There are literally hundreds of tarot decks available, but where do you start your shopping? Many people will go to their local chain bookstore. Keep in mind, though, that selection will be limited mostly to "bestsellers." It may very well be that your first deck will be one of these, but you may want to take advantage of other venues to shop around. A good place to start is a metaphysical or New Age bookstore. Because they are more focused on spiritual exploration, they may have a larger, more diverse selection of cards and a more informed sales staff.

Most people would prefer to look at an entire deck before purchasing. This is not always possible, especially in larger chain stores. Smaller specialty stores may have samples of cards or even sample decks available for you to peruse. If not, see if they offer classes. Many teachers have large collections of decks. Sometimes teachers offer free introductory classes that allow you to browse their collections. Ask your local store if they have such a class. If they don't offer it, encourage them to. It is a great way for beginners to see many decks and to see if they are interested in more classes by that teacher. If there are no classes, try to find a local group of tarot enthusiasts and attend one of their meetings.

If you can't find a store that will show you all the cards of a particular deck—or if you can't find a store with a good selection—you can request a catalog from a tarot card publisher such as Llewellyn Publications or U.S. Games. The catalogs will give you an overview of what the publisher offers, a brief description of the deck, and a few color pictures of some of the cards. The Internet is another great way to research different decks. You can find reviews and pictures of decks. Some tarot deck artists have their own websites where you can learn more and see more pictures. One particularly useful site is tarotpassages.com. There you can find extensive reviews and more images from various decks.

Overview of Decks

Here we'll briefly review a variety of decks. This overview will help you begin your search for the perfect deck for you. If something is called a kit, it includes a deck and a full-size book. A minikit contains a deck and a small book. A deck includes a little white booklet with brief divinatory meanings for the cards. Assume that Wands are associated with Fire and Swords with Air, unless otherwise noted.

Buckland Romani Tarot kit
by
Ray Buckland, art by Lissanne Lake

Although there is little historic evidence supporting the theory, many people believe that the Rom (Gypsies) introduced the tarot to Europe. Whether or not you accept this, if you enjoy the mystique of the Rom culture or have an interest in learning more about them, this deck is an authentic portrayal of their culture. The art is rich and the cards largely follow the Rider-Waite tradition.

Card size: 2¾ x 4½"

Suggested use: divination

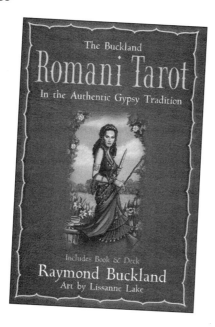

The Celtic Dragon Tarot kit
by
D. J. Conway, art by Lisa Hunt

The tarot is closely related to the elements (Earth, Air, Fire, Water, Spirit). Dragons, whether you believe them to exist in some fashion or consider them metaphors, are also connected with the use of elemental energies. This elegantly drawn deck is illustrated in the Rider-Waite tradition, except that Wands are associated with Air and Swords are associated with Fire. In addition, the book includes instructions for candle magic.

Card size: 2¾ x 4½"

Suggested uses: divination and/or magic

Legend: The Arthurian Tarot (available as a deck or kit)
by
Anna-Marie Ferguson

This deck is a natural choice for a lover of Arthurian legends. This exquisite deck and text was written and painted by Arthurian expert Anna-Marie Ferguson. The deck somewhat follows the Rider-Waite tradition. It is best suited for someone who either already knows the legends or has a very strong interest in learning them.

Card size: 2¾ x 4½"

Suggested uses: divination, meditation, journaling

The Nigel Jackson Tarot minikit
by
Nigel Jackson

British artist Nigel Jackson created this breathtaking deck with art derived from medieval engraving and woodcuts, Rhenish tapestry, and the art of Dürer, Holbein, and Schongauer. The colors are rich and bright. Jackson breaks from the Rider-Waite tradition, basing his deck's structure on magic Pythagorean numerology. It comes with a useful book, which is a good thing. While it is suitable for beginners, books based on the Rider-Waite tradition would be less useful with this deck. Wands are Air and Swords are Fire in this deck. Don't let the phrase "Pythagorean numerology" put you off—Jackson makes it quite easy.

Card size: 3⅓ x 5"

Suggested use: divination

The Quest Tarot kit
by
Joseph Ernest Martin

Joseph Martin makes the tarot accessible to beginners with this visually exciting deck. The images themselves are magical and inviting, allowing much scope for the imagination. It is also filled with helpful and fun extras, like the ability to spell out answers (rather like a Ouija board), a simple way to answer yes/no questions, and the incorporation of astrological, Kabbalistic, runic, I Ching, and gemstone correspondences. The deck features two extra cards: The Multiverse and a blank card.

Card size: 2¾ x 4½"

Suggested use: divination, meditation, magic

The Robin Wood Tarot deck
by
Robin Wood

This is an incredibly popular deck, because of its beautiful illustrations and because it is an excellent alternative for Pagans and non-Pagans who do not connect with the Christian-symbol-laden Rider-Waite deck. Wood follows the Rider-Waite tradition but substitutes more accessible symbolism. You could use most any beginner book in conjunction with these cards.

Card size: 2¾ x 4½"

Suggested use: divination

The Sacred Circle Tarot kit
by
Anna Franklin, art by Paul Mason

Like the *Robin Wood Tarot*, this deck is popular with those wanting an alternative to Christian symbolism. While the Minor Arcana cards are not illustrated in the Rider-Waite tradition, it is still a good choice for beginners because of its stunning images and Celtic basis. It is particularly suited for meditation and spiritual exploration.

Card size: 3⅓ x 5"

Suggested uses: meditation, magic, divination

The Shapeshifter Tarot kit
by
D. J. Conway and Sirona Knight, art by Lisa Hunt

Based on the Celtic shamanic art of shapeshifting, this deck explores animal and elemental energies. Hunt's illustrations are detailed and mystical. This may not be the best choice for divination for a beginner, but it would be an excellent choice for magical and spiritual work. Wands are Air, Swords are Fire.

Card size: 2¾ x 4½"

Suggested uses: magic, spiritual readings, divination

The Shining Tribe Tarot kit
by
Rachel Pollack

Rachel Pollack is one of the most celebrated tarot scholars of our time. Her approach to the tarot is playful and deep, brilliantly simple and astonishing complex. The images in this deck are hardly Rider-Waite clones but are based on that tradition. This probably isn't the best choice for a beginner's divination deck, but it is an exceptional deck for spiritual work.

Card size: 2¾ x 4½"

Suggested uses: spiritual readings, meditation, divination

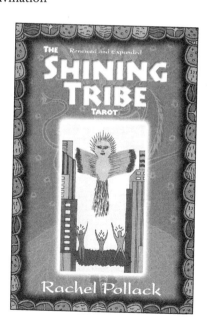

The Ship of Fools Tarot kit
by
Brian Williams

Like Rachel Pollack, Brian Williams was one of the most prolific and celebrated tarot designers of our time. His sad and untimely death occurred as this book was going to press. Based on the work of the medieval German poet Sebastian Brant, this deck is whimsical and fun, yet also sophisticated in its discussion of the foolish. The book is useful to beginners because it traces the evolution of card images from the Marseilles deck to the Rider-Waite to his own deck. Probably not a good first deck, but consider it for a second deck.

Card size: 3 x 4½"
Suggested uses: divination, meditation

The Tarot of Oz minikit
by
David Sexton

There is more to the Oz mythology than the movie tells. In L. Frank Baum's series of Oz books, he creates a timeless archetypal journey that is perfectly suited to the tarot. Suggested as a first deck only if you are familiar with the Oz mythology. Sexton's illustrations are bright, colorful, and charming.

Card size: 3 x 4½"

Suggested use: divination

Tarot of the Saints kit
by
Robert M. Place

This exceptionally beautiful deck would be an excellent first deck for someone well grounded in the history of the Christian saints or with an interest in gnosticism. Place follows the Rider-Waite tradition.

Card size: 2¾ x 4½"

Suggested use: divination

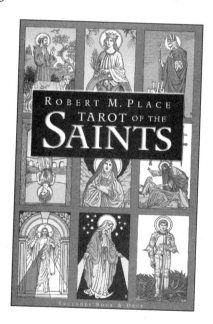

Victoria Regina Tarot kit
by
Sarah Ovenall and George Patterson,
art by Sarah Ovenall

Ovenall is a master collage artist and uses her Victorian source material to great effect. Knowledge of Victorian history is not necessary to use this deck, although, of course, an interest in the time period and an appreciation for its style are essential. The collages follow the Rider-Waite tradition.

Card size: 3⅓ x 5⅔"

Suggested use: divination

Waking the Wild Spirit Tarot kit
by
Poppy Palin

Palin takes a nontraditional and creative approach to the tarot. Standard card images and names are replaced with those of her Wildwitch tradition. In the accompanying book, the characters in each card speak directly to us through a first-person narrative that brings the archetypes to life in astonishing detail. Although vivid, colorful, and engaging, this is probably not the best choice for a beginning divination deck. However, it would be good for meditation and spiritual work.

Card size: 3 x 4½″

Suggested uses: meditation, spiritual work

The Witches Tarot deck
by
Ellen Cannon Reed, art by Martin Cannon

Here is another alternative for Pagans or non-Pagans desiring a deck without Christian symbolism. This is a strictly Pagan deck that introduces the use of the Kabbalistic system. While not discussed in this book, the Kabbalistic Tree of Life is an important part of many people's tarot and spiritual practice. The colorful, fantasy-style art goes to the edges of the cards, making it a favorite for meditation work.

Card size: 2¾ x 4½"

Suggested uses: meditation, spiritual work, divination

The World Spirit Tarot minikit
by
Lauren O'Leary and Jessica Godino,
art by Lauren O'Leary

This deck is a wonderful choice for those looking for something based on the Rider-Waite tradition without the Christian symbolism. O'Leary's art expresses a modern, multicultural, inclusive sensibility. The art is stunning, creative, and bright; the book is concise and useful. This deck is one of the author's favorites and is recommended highly as a first deck, assuming that the art appeals to you.

Card size: 3 x 4½"

Suggested uses: divination, meditation

Universal Tarot deck
by
De Angelis

For those interested in the Rider-Waite deck but looking for illustrations with a more sophisticated use of composition and color, this is a good one to consider.

Card size: 2¾ x 4½"

Suggested use: appropriate for all uses

Epilogue

Throughout this book we've read lots of examples from the lives of many people. We have spent quite a bit of time with Leslie and Tom, the couple who have been happy for two years and now find themselves at a crossroads. You have a little information about their personalities and what they want at this point. You know that they are going to meet in two weeks time to re-evaluate their relationship. You know that, in the meantime, Leslie is continuing to work with the cards. You do not know what Tom is doing.

We usually like our stories concluded. We yearn for resolution. So what is going to happen with Leslie and Tom? Unfortunately, you will not find out in these pages. Fortunately, this provides you with a wonderful opportunity. You must write the ending. Use their case study as a way to practice your own skills. Think about what each might be doing in the two weeks to come. Think about what they will talk about when they meet. Will Leslie try some tarot magic? Will Tom go to a professional reader? Will Leslie devise a spread for them to do together? Decide for yourself. Then write out the spell that Leslie might try, do the reading for Tom yourself, or create and interpret a spread that they work on together. If you are at a loss, then let the cards themselves tell the story. Shuffle and lay out five random cards and read them as a narrative. You might find it a little frightening to lay the cards for yourself or your friends at first, but doing these exercises, with Tom and Leslie as the subjects, will be a safe, stress-free, and maybe even fun way to practice your skills.

Card Meanings

For two reasons, this list is only a basic guide. First, you will develop your own interpretations of the cards. Second, decks vary. The image on the card from your deck may not match the interpretation given here. Like all the suggestions in this book—indeed like the tarot itself—these interpretations are open to adaptation and revision.

The Major Arcana

The Fool: represents beginnings of a grand adventures, being at the crossroads, innocence

The Magician: represents conscious use of power, confidence in skills, creative ability

The High Priestess: represents secret knowledge and mystery, the need to pay attention to your subconscious/dreams

The Empress: represents abundance, nature, nurturing, fertility

The Emperor: represents authority, structure, stability, leadership

The Hierophant: represents formal education or belief systems, societal norms, traditions

The Lovers: represents being faced with a choice, relationships, romance

The Chariot: represents self-control, will, achievement

Strength: represents strength, self-control, compassion, calmness

The Hermit: represents introspection, solitude, finding inner peace and truth

Wheel of Fortune: represents fate, change

Justice: represents karma, justice, personal responsibility

The Hanged Man: represents sacrifice, reversal of situation, adopting a different perspective

Death: represents transition, ending, transformation

Temperance: represents balance, grace under pressure, alchemy

The Devil: represents bondage, temptations, addictions

The Tower: represents unexpected change, revelation

Star: represents hope, optimism, inspiration, faith

The Moon: represents illusions, dreams, fantasies, deepest fears

The Sun: represents vitality, success, pleasure

Judgement: represents higher callings, rebirth, thinking outside the box

The World: represents integration, fulfillment, liberation

The Minor Arcana

wands

Ace: represents creative force, new beginnings

Two: represents initiative

Three: represents foresight

Four: represents celebration

Five: represents competition, disagreement

Six: represents victory

Seven: represents conviction

Eight: represents fast-moving events

Nine: represents defensiveness

Ten: represents excessive burdens

Page: is enthusiastic

Knight: is passionate, adventurous, brave, can be reckless

Queen: is energetic, confident

King: is inspiring, charismatic

cups

Ace: represents emotional energy, new beginnings

Two: represents union, partnership, often romantic

Three: represents friendship, joy of life

Four: represents apathy, discontentment

Five: represents loss, mourning

Six: represents nostalgia, romanticizing something

Seven: represents fantasies, distractions, options

Eight: represents searching

Nine: represents satisfaction, wishes fulfilled

Ten: represents family/domestic happiness, joy

Page: is emotional, can be intuitive

Knight: is romantic, dreamy, sensitive, can be lazy

Queen: is loving, intuitive, creative

King: is calm, devoted, patron of arts

swords

Ace: represents intellectual ability, new beginnings

Two: represents truce, refusal to acknowledge problems

Three: represents heartbreak

Four: represents rest, recuperation, temporary escape

Five: represents dishonor, deceit

Six: represents travel, leaving troubled waters

Seven: represents sneakiness, deceptiveness

Eight: represents feeling powerless and bound

Nine: represents intense worry, depression, nightmares

Ten: represents end of a difficult cycle

Page: is truthful, can be blunt

Knight: is logical, authoritative, can be unfeeling

Queen: is honest, sharp witted, harsh, a good organizer

King: is analytical, rational, gives good advice

pentacles

Ace: represents material or physical force, new beginnings

Two: represents balance, flexibility

Three: represents working together, creating

Four: represents control, fear, selfishness

Five: represents poverty, hard times

Six: represents charity, controlling resources

Seven: represents assessment of investments

Eight: represents attention to detail, skilled worker

Nine: represents achievement through discipline, self-reliance

Ten: represents affluence, enjoyment of achievements

Page: is practical, applies self to task at hand

Knight: is diligent, cautious, can be boring

Queen: is nurturing, resourceful, creative

King: is generous, industrious, enjoys the fruit of his labors

Glossary

Arcana: Arcana comes from the Latin word *arcanus*, meaning secrets or mysterious knowledge. See also **MAJOR ARCANA** and **MINOR ARCANA**.

Archetype: From Jungian psychological terminology, an archetype is an inherited pattern of thought or symbolism derived from the past collective experience and present in the individual unconscious.

Court cards: The catch-all phrase for the four high cards in the **MINOR ARCANA**, generally called individually King, Queen, Knight, and Page. These cards are found in each suit. They are sometimes called by other names, for example Father, Mother, Son, Daughter. Even renamed, they are still referred to as the court cards.

Layout: See **SPREAD**.

Major Arcana: The first twenty-two cards of the tarot, numbered zero through twenty-one. Literally "major secrets." These cards generally refer to large, spiritual, or milestone-like events in the QUERENT'S life. See also ARCANA.

Minor Arcana: The Ace through Ten and court cards of the four suits, totaling fifty-six cards. Literally "minor secrets." These cards generally refer to everyday occurrences. See also ARCANA.

Pip cards: In traditional playing cards, the Aces through Tens have an arrangement of abstract symbols representing their respective SUITS. These symbols are called pips. Although Aces through Tens that have scenes on them are not technically pip cards, they are still sometimes referred to as such.

Querent: The person asking the question of the tarot. Sometimes referred to as the seeker.

Reading: The act of phrasing a question and then shuffling, spreading, and interpreting the cards.

Reversals: When a card appears in a spread upside down (the top of the image is at the bottom as you look at it).

Seeker: See QUERENT.

Significator: A card chosen (in any manner of methods) to represent the QUERENT in reading.

Spread: The pattern in which the cards are placed. Each position has a meaning such as "Past," "Present," "Future," or "Outcome." Also called a layout.

Suits: The four sets of cards numbered Ace through Ten and court cards, generally named Wands, Cups, Swords, and Pentacles.

Suggested Reading

Basic divination

Abraham, Sylvia. *How to Read the Tarot: The Keyword System.*

A very easy and effective keyword system for reading tarot cards. Includes a few spreads and sample readings.

Abraham, Sylvia. *How to Use Tarot Spreads.*

A collection of thirty-seven predesigned tarot spreads covering such topics as love, romance, family, money, milestone decisions, and spiritual development. Includes basic interpretations from *How to Read the Tarot.*

Hollander, P. Scott. *Tarot for Beginners: An Easy Guide to Understanding & Interpreting the Tarot.*

A solid beginner book with in-depth interpretation, spreads, and sample readings.

Louis, Anthony. *Tarot Plain and Simple.*

A good beginner book featuring keywords and phrases for each card as well as guidance for interpreting the cards as either situations or people.

Porter, Tracy. *Tarot Companion: An Essential Reference Guide.*

A good reference guide that includes correspondences between the tarot and numerology, astrology, Kabbala, I Ching, runes, and chakras. Also includes information on card combinations, timing, and common symbols in tarot cards.

Renée, Janina. *Tarot for a New Generation.*

Although geared for teens and twenty-somethings, this book is excellent for beginners of all ages. It includes interpretations for specific situations such as character, romance, travel, education, relationships, and other topics. The appendices provide information on significator cards and incorporating color symbolism in your readings.

Renée, Janina. *Tarot: Your Everyday Guide.*

Very in-depth interpretations for each card. Features a unique yet simple way of reading the cards for problem solving and advice.

Ricklef, James. *Tarot Tells the Tale.*

This is a very unique and exciting book. First, it provides enough information for a beginner to perform readings. Second, it explores many uses for three-card readings, which are often easier for beginners. It even breaks down the Celtic Cross spread into a series of three-card spreads, making that spread much easier to interpret effectively. Finally, it teaches how to perform an integrated, useful reading through sample readings for figures from literature, history, fairy tales, and mythology. This book is not only very educational, it is also a very entertaining read.

Intermediate & Advanced Readers

Amber K and Azrael K. *Heart of Tarot: An Intuitive Approach.*

This book teaches how to read the cards using the Gestalt method, a technique that focuses on accessing the subconscious rather than relying on consciously determined or memorized meanings. Also included: chapters on tarot magic, teaching tarot, and reading cards professionally.

Jette, Christine. *Professional Tarot: The Business of Reading, Consulting, and Teaching.*

The first book ever dedicated to the needs of the professional reader. Whether you are just considering becoming a pro or have been reading professionally for years, this book has something for you: developing your niche as a reader, marketing, record keeping, teaching classes, and avoiding psychic burnout.

Jette, Christine. *Tarot for the Healing Heart: Using Inner Wisdom to Heal Mind & Body.*

Techniques for using tarot cards to facilitate health and healing.

Jette, Christine. *Tarot Shadow Work: Using the Dark Symbols to Heal.*

A program designed to explore and integrate your shadow-self to create a healthy life.

McElroy, Mark. *Putting the Tarot to Work.*

Exciting and accessible techniques for using the tarot in your work life. Learn brainstorming and problem-solving techniques, prepare for reviews, and create a winning résumé.

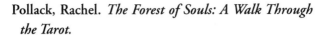

Pollack, Rachel. *The Forest of Souls: A Walk Through the Tarot.*

A unique work by a well-known and respected tarot expert. This book explores the fun and the spiritual aspects of the cards.

Sterling, Stephen. *Tarot Awareness: Exploring the Spiritual Path.*

An essential guide for those using the tarot as a guide on their spiritual path. Includes spiritual interpretation and direction for effective meditations.

Wiccan/Magic

Jette, Christine. *Tarot for All Seasons: Celebrating the Days and Nights of Power.*

Use the tarot to enhance your lunar and solar celebrations of the Wheel of the Year.

Morrison, Dorothy. *Everyday Tarot Magic: Meditation & Spells.*

A collection of spells all using the tarot. Includes beginner information and a section about using the cards for self-discovery.

Moura, Ann. *Tarot for the Green Witch.*

Interprets the cards in a way that honors earth-based spirituality, emphasizes elemental and numerological aspects of the cards and the relationships between the cards.

Renée, Janina. *Tarot Spells.*

A collection of tarot-based spells and information on performing effective magic.

Special Topics

Llewellyn Publication's Special Topics in Tarot series was created to provide readers with in-depth information on specific subjects or techniques. These books do not cover basic beginner material. Written by experts with practical experience, these books can enhance and expand your tarot practice.

Amberstone, Ruth Ann and Wald. *Tarot Tips.*

A collection of useful tips on a variety of topics, including interpretation, spreads, reading techniques, and ethics.

Braden, Nina Lee. *Tarot for Self-Discovery.*

An excellent collection of beginner, intermediate, and special-occasion exercises for using the tarot in the process of self-discovery and advice on how to create your own exercises.

Gillentine, Julie. *Tarot & Dream Interpretation.*

Easy and effective techniques for working with your dreams and using the tarot to interpret them.

Greer, Mary K. *The Complete Book of Tarot Reversals.*

The only book you'll ever need for understanding working with reversed cards. You'll learn different theories about reversals, allowing you to determine the one you want to work with.

Kraig, Donald M. *Tarot & Magic.*

Everything you need to know to start using magic and tarot to change your life, including spell work, rituals, and talismans.

Michelsen, Teresa. *Designing Your Own Tarot Spreads.*

Learn how to ask a perfect question and then design a spread to answer it. Includes information on reversals, dignities, significators, and clarification cards.

Other Useful Books

Clement, Stephanie. *Meditation for Beginners: Techniques for Awareness, Mindfulness, & Relaxation.*

An excellent guide for those wanting to learn more about meditation.

Lorenzo-Fuentes, Jose. *Meditation.*

A short introductory work covering several types of meditation.

Morrison, Dorothy. *Everyday Magic: Spells and Rituals for Modern Living.*

A good reference book for magical workings. Includes magical properties of herbs and stones, a list of deities and their magical connections, as well as basic information about magic and a collection of useful, simple spells.

Trobe, Kala. *Magic of Qabalah: Visions of the Tree of Life.*

Learn about the Kabbala, pathworking, the Tree of Life, and the Kabbala's connection with tarot. Also includes meditations and visualizations.

Webster, Richard. *Write Your Own Magic: The Hidden Power in Your Words.*

Explores the power of words and how to harness that power through writing. This book would be useful in expanding your journaling work with the tarot.

All titles mentioned in this book are published by Llewellyn Publications, St. Paul, Minnesota, and are available at www.llewellyn.com.

☽ REACH FOR THE MOON

Llewellyn publishes hundreds of books on your favorite subjects! To get these exciting books, including the ones on the following pages, check your local bookstore or order them directly from Llewellyn.

Order by Phone
- Call toll-free within the U.S. and Canada, 1-877-NEW-WRLD
- In Minnesota, call (651) 291-1970
- We accept VISA, MasterCard, and American Express

Order by Mail
- Send the full price of your order (MN residents add 7% sales tax) in U.S. funds, plus postage & handling to:
  Llewellyn Worldwide
  P.O. Box 64383, Dept. 0-7387-0173-4
  St. Paul, MN 55164–0383, U.S.A.

Postage & Handling
- **Standard** (U.S., Mexico, & Canada) If your order is:
  $20 or under, add $5
  $20.01–$100, add $6
  Over $100, shipping is free
(Continental U.S. orders ship UPS. AK, HI, PR, & P.O. Boxes ship USPS 1st class. Mex. & Can. ship PMB.)
- **Second Day Air** (Continental U.S. only): $10 for one book plus $1 per each additional book
- **Express** (AK, HI, & PR only) [Not available for P.O. Box delivery. For street address delivery only.]: $15 for one book plus $1 per each additional book
- **International Surface Mail:** $20 or under, add $5 plus $1 per item; $20.01 and over, add $6 plus $1 per item
- **International Airmail:** Books—Add the retail price of each item; Non-book items—Add $5 per item

Please allow 4–6 weeks for delivery on all orders.
Postage and handling rates subject to change.

Discounts
We offer a 20% discount to group leaders or agents. You must order a minimum of 5 copies of the same book to get our special quantity price.

FREE CATALOG
Get a free copy of our color catalog, *New Worlds of Mind and Spirit.* Subscribe for just $10.00 in the United States and Canada ($30.00 overseas, airmail). Call 1-877-NEW-WRLD today!

Visit our website at www.llewellyn.com for more information.

To Write to the Author

If you wish to contact the author or would like more information about this book, please write to the author in care of Llewellyn Worldwide and we will forward your request. Both the author and publisher appreciate hearing from you and learning of your enjoyment of this book and how it has helped you. Llewellyn Worldwide cannot guarantee that every letter written to the author can be answered, but all will be forwarded. Please write to:

Barbara Moore
⁒ Llewellyn Worldwide
P.O. Box 64383, Dept. 0-7387-0173-4
St. Paul, MN 55164-0383, U.S.A.

Please enclose a self-addressed stamped envelope for reply, or $1.00 to cover costs. If outside U.S.A., enclose international postal reply coupon.

Many of Llewellyn's authors have websites with additional information and resources. For more information, please visit our website at www.llewellyn.com.